Family Sunday School Fun

Group
Loveland, Colorado

Family Sunday School Fun

Copyright © 1999 Tim Smith

Visit our Web site: **www.grouppublishing.com**

Credits

Contributing Authors: Janis Kraushaar, Mike Sciarra, and Tim Smith
General Editor: Tim Smith
Editors: Paul Allen, Debbie Gowensmith, Jim Kochenburger, Julie Meiklejohn, and Jennifer Wilger
Creative Development Editor: Dave Thornton
Chief Creative Officer: Joani Schultz
Copy Editor: Bob Kretschman
Art Director: Jean Bruns
Cover Art Director: Jeff A. Storm
Cover Designer: Diana Walters
Computer Graphic Artist: Joyce Douglas
Production Manager: Peggy Naylor

Library of Congress Cataloging-in-Publication Data
Family Sunday school fun.
    p. cm.
  ISBN 0-7644-2122-0 (alk. paper)
   1. Bible--Study and teaching (Elementary)--Activity Programs. 2. Family--Religious life.
3. Christian education of children. I. Group Publishing.
  BS618 .F35 1999
249--dc21   99-31156
                                                                          CIP

Printed in the United States of America.

Contents

Introduction

Congratulations! You have in your hands a tool that can help you act as a pioneer in your church—someone on the cutting edge! It's so cutting-edge that you may not be familiar with it. It's the idea of learning together—*kids and parents learning together!* You have the unique opportunity to lay the foundation for one of the newest approaches in Christian education—families together for Sunday school!

For many years, the typical approach to Christian education has often been to separate families into two distinct groups—kids and parents. This comes from the idea that people learn best when they are with their peers. While this may be true for many subjects, it definitely isn't true within the realm of spiritual growth. In order for families to grow *together* spiritually, they need to learn *together* spiritual truths.

Together—this is the key word. People living in today's culture are busier than ever, and they're desperate for quality family time. It's ironic that many churches place family spiritual growth at a high priority but then split up family groups every time they're in church. *Family Sunday School Fun* will bring your families together.

All the wonderfully helpful programs offered by the church are to supplement what's done within the family. What a child learns at church should complement what he or she is learning at home. In reality, kids and parents interacting with spiritual truths together is a concept that is three thousand years old! Consider this truth from Scripture:

"These commandments that I give you today are to be upon your hearts. Impress them on your children. Talk about them when you sit at home and when you walk along the road, when you lie down and when you get up. Tie them as symbols on your hands and bind them on your foreheads. Write them on the doorframes of your houses and on your gates" (Deuteronomy 6:6-9).

As parents walk and talk, as they lie down and get up, they are to make every effort to impress God's commandments on their children. The responsibility for children's spiritual development in the child's younger years lies primarily with their parents. *Family Sunday School Fun* will equip parents to live out Deuteronomy 6:6-9.

Family Sunday School Fun provides a tool to begin to create a partnership between home and church. It's a flexible series that can be used in a variety of settings. It's designed to help parents assume the responsibility of helping their kids grow spiritually. It gives them tools and experiences that will enhance spiritual growth. It's designed to be a bridge between what happens at church and what happens at home. It's also designed to be a bridge between parents and children.

Family Sunday School Fun is:

• **Interactive**—It's designed to promote activity and discussion between kids and their parents.

• **Intergenerational**—It's written with the goal of mixing generations: parents with children; grandparents with grandchildren; maybe even three generations. The idea behind *Family Sunday School Fun* is to learn and have fun together.

• **Inclusive**—Everyone is welcome! There are so many types of families today: single-parent families, blended families, multigenerational families, and two-parent families. *Family Sunday School Fun* seeks to include all kinds of families.

Here are typical lesson components:

• **Gathering Activity**—This activity creatively introduces the session theme and gets participants involved and engaged right away, whether they are young or old.

• **Bible Story Time**—In this activity, family groups creatively explore and often experience the Scripture.

• **Family Learning Activity**—Family groups experience the theme and make general application in a fun, active way. As a group they process and apply the theme together through discussion.

• **Covenant Time**—Family groups apply the lesson focus to their lives and then close in a prayer of commitment.

• **Optional Snack Time**—The group shares in a delicious snack that's related to the lesson's theme.

• **"For Younger Kids" and "For Older Kids" boxes**—Activities in each session are geared toward adults with kids aged seven through nine. These boxes provide adaptation tips and ideas for younger (ages five to six) or older kids (ages ten to eleven) as necessary.

• **"Field-Test Findings" boxes**—Each session was field tested with real kids and parents. These boxes provide helpful tips from these tests.

Also, it may be helpful to have participants evaluate each session. This provides valuable feedback for use in future sessions. Use the "Evaluation Form" (p. 125) for this purpose.

We're excited about the revolutionary potential of intergenerational Sunday school. Thanks for being courageous and pioneering with us by using *Family Sunday School Fun*!

TIPS FOR USING *FAMILY SUNDAY SCHOOL FUN*

If your church is like most churches, it has never attempted intergenerational Sunday school with an exceedingly high level of vision, energy, or resources. Perhaps there is a past failure to institute this bold approach in your church. That's OK—the past is past, and besides, they didn't have *Family Sunday School Fun* to help them along the way back then. You do, so bravely forge ahead.

Even being the bold pioneer that you are, you may need to recalibrate some things in your mind or certainly in the minds of those who will actually teach this course. Why? For the simple fact that adults (parents) and their children are different. You have two very different kinds of participants involved in family Sunday school, and both are very used to Sunday school as they know it. In this article, read just a few key ways kids and their parents are different and how *Family Sunday School Fun* can help you meet the needs of both.

Different Roles

The parents in your class are accustomed to filling a role as an adult during Sunday school, but most will not be used to carrying the additional role and responsibility of "parent" for their children in the Sunday school class. Some do not want to supervise their children during this time and may come across as a little impatient with their kids or maybe a little strong on their correction. As a leader, you can do several things to help. Consider having some child-care personnel supervise the children in a play area of the classroom during the first part of your lesson, allowing parents to socialize and lifting the supervision burden a bit. Assist adults in supervising their children.

Different Environment

The question of environment comes quickly to the fore when we are talking about parents and children together in a classroom. Though the design and construction of the typical church sanctuary is meant to invite adult participation, the wise leader of a family Sunday school class will cater more to the kids than the adults. Why? Adults, with their maturity, can more easily adapt to an unfamiliar setting that pushes them out of their comfort zone.

Establish the environment in a number of ways. Play children's music as everyone arrives. Decorate the class as you would a classroom for children. Hold this class in a classroom normally used by children (but offer an adequate number of adult-sized chairs). *Family Sunday School Fun* caters a little more to the children than the adults in most of its activities, but adults should find the activities to be inclusive and interesting and the discussions engaging.

Different Lesson Style

In the typical adult Sunday school class, adults sit and listen to a study read or presented in lecture style by a leader. These classes are often information-oriented. There may or may not be discussion. (That is, if they are not using Group's Apply-It-To-Life™ Adult Bible Curriculum, which is fun, features activities, and promotes interaction.) Kids, on the other hand, are used to activity-based, discovery-oriented, fun, and interactive lessons, particularly if their teachers are using Group's Hands-On Bible Curriculum™ or FaithWeaver™ resources.

It will take adults a little while to adjust to the fun, interactive, and activity-based lessons of *Family Sunday School Fun*. Still, during the Bible Story Time section of the lesson in which the Bible story is explored and emphasized, the approach is less active and more information-based. This approach should be palatable to the adults and not uncomfortable for the kids.

Different Energy Levels and Attention Spans

Adults can do just fine sitting straight up in their chairs and quietly listening to a lesson as it is taught. They can do this for hours (well, maybe not hours). Kids have got to get up and move around, share, talk, and laugh a little bit during class, or it just wouldn't be natural. This is where parents may tend to overcorrect their children, not understanding

TIPS FOR LEADING DISCUSSIONS

These tips are provided because adults are often called upon in *Family Sunday School Fun* to lead their own families in discussion. These adults may not be experienced discussion leaders. These pointers should help them.

• **Don't feel a burden to talk.** It is far better when leading a discussion to listen to others and then clarify and restate what you heard them say. Avoid the temptation to lecture.

• **Realize that most of the questions in the discussions you will lead are open-ended** questions so family members can enjoy a free exchange of ideas. There is no "right" answer to these questions; the goal is for everyone to share freely.

• **Avoid criticizing others' opinions or forcing your own opinions.** Openness and security are important to the success of your discussions. The goal isn't necessarily to agree, but to discuss.

(continued on next page)

• Be enthusiastic! The attitude is contagious. It keeps away the deadly "This-is-stupids" and "I-don't-wanna's."

• Don't fear silence or the tension that will inevitably arise from discussing certain topics. Silence offers people a chance to reflect on what someone has said or to reconsider their own positions on an issue.

• Enjoy yourself! If you have fun, it's more likely others will too. Savor this time together.

the difference and that the difference is OK. Help everyone by keeping the lesson pace moving quickly from activity to activity. Be enthusiastic about the activities to help spur adults to be enthusiastic as well.

Different Tastes

You know how earlier it was stated to decorate the room for kids and to play kids' music? Well, you don't want to orient toward kids when it comes down to refreshments served. Low- or no-sugar cookies and juice may be great for the kids, but adults must have the coffee-and-doughnut-type stuff. First, have refreshments. Families can pair up and take turns supplying these each week. Second, consider setting up the adult coffee and doughnut area just outside your classroom door. This keeps the coffee maker from becoming a safety hazard inside the room where a child may inadvertently knock it over, and this also keeps kids from seeing adults (who can tolerate the sugar) enjoying doughnuts the kids cannot (because they may end up "bouncing off the walls" from the sugar).

Different Socialization

Adults will likely come into the classroom and stand with their friends, calmly discussing the matters of the day. Kids come ready to play, so they must have a program going right away. Have coloring pages and crayons and markers available. Have a video playing. Consider having one or two parents take turns volunteering each week to lead kids in a ten- to fifteen-minute activity at the beginning of the class. These volunteers can be given Group books such as *Friend Makers & Crowd Breakers for Children's Ministry* for ideas of what to do with the kids during this time.

There are other differences between children and adults, but those in this article are perhaps the most important to address. During the first lesson, consider covering with all the participants this article and how this class will be different from their usual Sunday school class. Most of all, emphasize to all a key core value to us here at Group, which is that we have a fun, friendly, fair, and forgiving work environment. Challenge participants to make these their own values for the lessons of *Family Sunday School Fun* as well.

Road Trip
Abraham

LESSON FOCUS:

When we follow God, it can mean giving up some things, but it will lead to blessing.

OBJECTIVES:

Family members will
- consider all the things they love most about their home and family,
- identify with Abraham's feelings about leaving home to follow God,
- explore what it means for them to follow God more closely and to trust him more deeply, and
- commit to do at least one thing to more closely follow God and trust him more deeply.

STUFF YOU WILL NEED:

Smooth stones, construction paper, double-stick tape, children's and adults' scissors, pens, markers or crayons, old magazines with lots of pictures, glue sticks, "Leaving Home" handouts (p. 15), "My Treasure Chest" handouts (p. 16), chalk and a chalkboard.

GATHERING ACTIVITY

Heart to Home Name Tags

(up to 15 minutes)

Field-Test FINDINGS

At the first session, you may want to distribute a course outline that lists each lesson's date, topic, Scripture text, and items to bring from home. Refer to the outline at the conclusion of each lesson.

Gather everyone together, sitting around tables. Distribute construction paper and double-stick tape, scissors (age-appropriate), glue sticks, markers or crayons, and some old magazines.

Say: **Let's begin today by custom-designing our name tags in the shape of something each of us loves about our homes. For example, if you love to swing on the swing in your yard, tear or cut your name tag to look like a swing; if you love to play basketball in your driveway, tear or cut your name tag into the shape of a ball; if you like to bake, tear or cut the name tag into the shape of a cake or pan.** When people are finished, they should write their names on the name tags and glue on pictures from magazines (or draw pictures) to depict other things they like most about their homes and families.

Say: **Turn to two other people who are not in your family, and explain to them your name tag, letting them know what you like most about your home and family.** Have a few volunteers share their name tags and explanations for them with the group.

Then ask:

• **What are the three words that best describe your family?**

• **What is your favorite place at home? Why?**

• **Who can define "comfortable"? Where is the most comfortable place in your home?**

Say: **Our name tags featured the things we most treasure in our homes and families. In fact, for some of us, these are the things that make our house a home. Turn to the same two people you shared with earlier, and ask one another: "What would your home be like if you didn't have these things you depicted on your name tag?"** Give the group several minutes to share this with one another.

Say: **Today we'll learn that when we follow God, it can mean giving up what is comfortable or, in some cases, what we know and love. But when God asks us to leave these things behind, it is always so he can bless us even more and fulfill for us a promise, just as he did with Abram. We'll see that Abram believed God and trusted him. So must we. Let's look more closely at Abram's story.**

BIBLE STORY TIME

Leaving Home

(up to 15 minutes)

Have everyone separate into their families for this activity. Distribute the "Leaving Home" handout (p. 15).

Say: **Abram is one of the first men that God used. God asked Abram to trust him. If Abram did, God would bless him with his heart's desire. Look together as a family at Abram's story.**

Have families read Abram's story from Genesis 12:1-8. Then give families five minutes to write their responses to the questions on the handout based on their reading. Finally, have them discuss within their families the questions below. Either write the following questions on the chalkboard, or copy them for families and distribute them:

- **What did it cost Abram to trust and obey God?**
- **Why do you believe Abram obeyed God? worshipped God as he did?**
- **How did the promises God made to Abram motivate him?**
- **What can we learn from Abram and his trust in God? his obedience to God? his worship of God even when he had not yet received the promises of God?**

After five minutes or so, gain the attention of the group, and say: **Is it any wonder Abram (later Abraham) is called the father of our faith? What a tremendous example for us of faith and trust in God, of belief, of courage, and of what it means to have a relationship with God. And you know what the best part is? Each of us can have the same kind of relationship with God and receive the same kind of blessing that Abraham did. But to do so, we too must be willing to hear God and obey what he might ask us to do, even if that means leaving behind our home and those things that we have come to love and value most and those things with which we feel most comfortable. Let's look at some of those things now.**

FAMILY LEARNING ACTIVITY

My Treasure Chest

(up to 15 minutes)

Have families remain separate for the first part of this activity.

Distribute the "My Treasure Chest" handouts (p. 16) to everyone.

Gain everyone's attention, and say: **Imagine that all the things you love about your family and home could be put inside a big treasure trunk. What would those items be? Take three minutes to list them all on your handout.** Allow family members two to three minutes to complete the handout. Then have them share with one another what each wrote or the drawings they made on their handouts. Then have family members discuss in their families the following question:

• **Say you were asked to move with only your food, clothes, and one toy or precious possession. What one thing would you choose to take with you? Why?**

Now have everyone come together. Lead them in discussing the following questions:

• **How would you feel about leaving all the people you loved, the home you loved, and all your precious possessions?**

• **How would this make sense to do if God tells us to do it and if we are following him?**

• **Although God may not promise us children or the chance to be the father of a great nation, what might God promise us if he called us to leave as he called Abram to leave?**

• **How do you think God would take care of us if we left the home we know, the people we love, and the possessions we have? Why?**

Gain everyone's attention, and say: **I think we can all agree that if we had to leave our friends, family, homes, and possessions we love and value, it would be very difficult. Yet this is exactly what God was calling Abram to do, and this is exactly what he did. God asked him to leave it all to go to some distant place he didn't even know!**

So why did Abram go? He went to please God by obeying him. And he left because he had a promise from God. What was that promise? Have someone read Genesis 12:2, 7.

Say: **God promised Abram a big family. Abram didn't have any children, and God was talking about him being a father of a "nation." How could this be? Yet Abram followed God, even though he didn't know exactly how God would work out all the details. Little did he know God was going to perform a miracle and give him and his wife Sarai a child even though they were both very old and way beyond the child-bearing years. There is nothing impossible for**

God, Abram would learn. For us to follow God and trust him even to the point of leaving all we know and love, we must believe nothing is impossible for him. We must trust that he will only call us to leave our current blessing to go to a greater blessing.

COVENANT TIME

Rock Solid Commitment to Follow (up to 5 minutes)

Families should meet separately for this activity. Each family should sit in a circle. Distribute smooth stones and markers. Have family members use markers to write on their stones, "I choose to follow God." They should write their initial and the date on the rocks. Then have family members take their completed "My Treasure Chest" handouts and place them in a pile on the floor in the middle of their family circle. Have families discuss the questions below. Either write the following questions on the chalkboard, or copy them for all the families:

• **In what one way could our family as a whole trust God more and follow him more closely?**

• **What must we give up to follow God more closely?**

• **In what one way could you trust God more? follow God more closely?**

• **What one thing would you find most difficult to give up or leave behind in order to follow God more closely? (If this is on your handout, circle it; if not, add it to the handout, and circle it.)**

Say: **We're going to have a moment of silence.** During that time, have different family members pray, thanking God for his faithfulness in the past when they've trusted him. Family members should pray aloud, but only loud enough for their family to hear. Allow families one or two minutes to pray.

Say: **God doesn't ask us to do anything unless he gives us what we need to do it. When we follow God, it may be uncomfortable, but he will bless us beyond whatever we leave behind no matter what that might be.**

Consider what you have written on your completed "My Treasure Chest" handout. Are you are willing to leave all of that behind if necessary to follow God? If so, when we bow our heads to pray in just a moment, place your stone on top of the stack of handouts

Kids age seven and younger may not understand the idea of "leaving home." Help them think about it in terms of visiting their friends or going to grandma's for a night. Help them see that going to someplace different is uncomfortable because it is not what we are used to.

Also, let these young ones know that Abram is the same person as Abraham, the Bible person with whom they may be familiar (and the same one about which they sing the song "Father Abraham"). Let them know that later on, God changes Abram's name to Abraham.

Some children may be able to relate to going away with a camp experience. Discuss with them what they couldn't take to camp. Were they more comfortable at camp or at home? What were some things they missed at camp? Discuss how the food and schedule would be different for a large group (like at camp). Usually the food isn't as good as it is at home, and the schedule is influenced by a lot of group activities. You don't have as much individual free time. What would it be like to live as if you are at camp with a million people?

in the middle of your family circle. In this way, you will make a family altar, a memorial of commitment to God, just as Abram, the father of our faith, did several thousand years ago. Let us bow our heads to pray...

Start families off in a prayer of commitment to follow God no matter what the cost, to obey him no matter what the command, and to trust him no matter how impossible the things may seem that he asks us to do. Have families close the prayer by praying as they desire within their family groups.

When everyone has finished praying, encourage family members to take their stones home and either keep them piled where they can easily be seen or for each to take his or her personal stone and keep it in a highly visible place in the home (such as a bedroom or the family room). This is to be a reminder of the commitment each made to follow God more closely and to trust him more deeply.

OPTIONAL SNACK TIME

Serve fruit leather or another kind of easy-to-carry food that you would take on a hike.

Another option is to have families make their own trail mix. Provide ingredients of granola, yogurt-covered raisins, raisins, M&M's candies, nuts, dried fruit, and other tasty trail mix supplies. Also provide resealable plastic bags. Have each family member select one ingredient based on something about the lesson: "Which of these trail mix ingredients best represents something about the lesson?" Invite them to share why they selected particular ingredients. After families have made their trail mix and put it in resealable plastic bags, encourage them to eat their snack.

Leaving Home

Genesis 12:1-8

Abram's family had lived in Haran for years. They had houses, cows, horses, sheep, and owned lots of land. The Lord told Abram to leave all he had ever known to follow him.

- **Why would it be hard to leave all of this stuff?**

As Abram traveled, he believed God and followed where God led him. As he went, he built altars to thank God and to worship him. An altar is something that is built to help people remember God and what he has done. An altar can be as simple as a pile of rocks or much more elaborate. The significant thing about altars is that they serve as memorials and reminders of God's goodness and faithfulness.

- **Why do you think Abram took the time to stop and worship God as he traveled?**

- **Why is it important for us to worship God?**

The Lord promised to make Abram's name great, to bless him with a large family, and to provide him with all that he needed. Abram did as God told him to do. And he was seventy-five years old!

- **What can seventy-five-year-olds easily do? What is difficult for them to do?**

- **How would this journey be hard for Abram at his age?**

My Treasure Chest

INSTRUCTIONS:

This is your treasure chest. In it are supposed to go all the things that you love most about your home and family. To put these things in your treasure chest, cover this page with as many of them as possible by either writing them down or drawing them—and be creative! If you have time, use markers to color in your treasure chest.

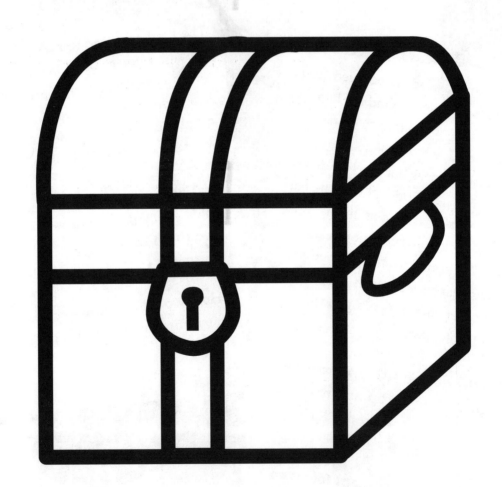

The Promised Son
Abraham and Isaac

LESSON FOCUS:

Sometimes God tests our faith to see if we truly trust him to keep his promises.

TEXT:
Genesis 21:1-8;
22:1-10; 22:11-18

OBJECTIVES:

Family members will
- experience and define what it means to trust and have faith;
- explore the depths of Abraham's faith and trust in God and be challenged in their own faith by it;
- realize that, just as God kept his promises to Abraham, so he also keeps his promises to us;
- make a family covenant to nurture a closer relationship between family members and God.

STUFF YOU WILL NEED:

One long, sturdy board (3x6); two concrete blocks; several blindfolds; "Definitions" handouts (p. 23); "God's Faithfulness" handouts (pp. 24-25), "God, the Promise Keeper" handouts (p. 26), "God's Promise Poster" handouts (p. 23), poster of a sky full of stars; one piece of 9x12 black poster board for each family; cup of sand; glue; blue cellophane; assorted star stickers (silver, gold, and glow-in-the-dark ones in various sizes), chalk (white or fluorescent yellow), paper; pens; chalk and a chalkboard, and glow-in-the-dark felt markers (optional).

GATHERING ACTIVITY

Walk by Faith

(up to 20 minutes)

Field-Test FINDINGS

Enlist any early arrivers to help you prepare for the session. You might also ask them to greet others as they arrive.

Before class, place a sturdy board across two concrete blocks to create a balance beam.

As people arrive, have them group around one end of the board.

Blindfold several people, and have them "walk by faith" on the balance beam in turn as their family members walk beside them on either side of the beam. The blindfolded people must trust family members to help them walk from one end of the board to the other without falling. Family members can offer the blindfolded walkers verbal advice to help them cross successfully but should not touch them. All family members should experience crossing the balance beam. As a variation, place the board on the floor and allow members of the family to walk on the board as they are led only by the voices of other family members. Ask:

• How did you feel as you crossed that balance beam blindfolded? Why?

• How was it easy or difficult to place your trust in your family during this "walk by faith"? Why?

• In real life, in what ways do you place your faith and trust in your family members?

Say: For those of you who did not hesitate to hustle across the balance beam, it was probably because you had faith and trusted your family members to keep you safe. Ask:

• Why were those of you who did not hesitate able to have that much faith in your family members?

Say: The purpose of the "walk by faith" exercise was to make us think about how much faith we have in others and in our Heavenly Father. Ask:

• What one word would you use to describe the depth of your faith and trust in God? Why?

Say: Let's define our terms and make sure everyone knows exactly what we will talk about today.

Field-Test FINDINGS

Consider having participants wear name tags to help people learn each other's names.

Definitions

(up to 5 minutes)

Have everyone try to guess the definitions of the following words:

faith, trust, obey, promise, sacrifice. Write on the chalkboard those that come closest to the correct definition. Then distribute to each person a copy of the "Definitions" handout (p. 23).

Say: **Just as the "walk by faith" we just participated in tested our faith in our family, God sometimes tests our faith in him.**

Today we will see that sometimes God tests our *faith* to see if we truly *trust* him to keep his *promises*. He tells us to *obey* him, sometimes asking us to *sacrifice* something. In the Bible story, God tests Abraham's faith by telling him to sacrifice (give back to God) something very precious to him. God wanted to see if Abraham trusted in his promise. Let's look at this Bible account today.

BIBLE STORY TIME

God's Faithfulness

(up to 20 minutes)

Families should meet separately for the beginning of this activity but will come together to present a special drama and discussion at the end. Distribute a copy of the "God's Faithfulness" handout (pp. 24-25) to each family. Assign families a letter: A, B, or C. The letter will determine which part of the handout each family will study and which team each family will be on. Families assigned to the A team will read Genesis 21:1-8 and write responses to those questions; while families assigned to the B team will read Genesis 22:1-10 and write responses to those questions; families assigned to the C team will read Genesis 22:11-18 and write responses to those questions. Families should complete the assignments working separately from other families.

When all have completed their assignments, families should join others on their team (A, B, or C). After everyone has gathered in their A, B, or C team, each team should select a narrator and actors to play all the parts in its study passage. Through narrated skit drama, each team will report the findings of its study to the large group. The narrator simply reads the summary in the "God's Faithfulness" handout (pp. 24-25) as the actors act it out. Narrator and actors should be encouraged to ham it up a bit.

After each group has presented its findings through drama, ask:

• **What were your thoughts and feelings as you studied and acted out this Bible account? Explain.**

• **What impressed you the most about Abraham's faith? Why?**

• In one word, how would you describe Abraham's faith?

• How would you compare your own faith in God with Abraham's? Why?

• Why do you think Abraham trusted God so deeply and sincerely?

• What most challenges you about Abraham's faith? Why?

Say: God's renewed promise told Abraham that he would have countless descendants because of his obedience and faithfulness. In Genesis 22:17, God even tells Abraham that his descendants will be "as numerous as the stars in the sky and as the sand on the seashore." How many are the descendants of Abraham? Infinity—including even us! Abraham's radical faith was rewarded beyond his wildest imagination.

Just as Abraham showed that he was willing to sacrifice his only son, Isaac, God showed that he was willing to sacrifice his only Son, Jesus Christ, so that we might live through him. Just as Isaac went willingly with his father, trusting that God would provide the lamb, Jesus submitted to God the Father by willingly going to the cross to die.

FAMILY LEARNING ACTIVITY

God, the Promise Keeper

(up to 20 minutes)

Have families work separately on the beginning of this activity and then come together at the end for a discussion.

If it is nighttime and it is a clear night, turn off the classroom lights and have everyone look out a window. Otherwise keep the classroom lights on and display a poster of a clear, starry night. Challenge everyone to try to count all the stars. After about thirty seconds, turn the lights back on or fold up the poster (so people will stop counting).

Say: Remember the promise God made to Abraham in Genesis 22:17 that he would make Abraham's descendants as numerous as the stars in the sky and the sand on the seashore? Every time Abraham saw the stars or looked down at the sand, surely he would be reminded of God's great and precious promises to him. Just as Abraham was reminded of God's great and precious promises to him, so are we now going to create something to remind us of God's great and precious promises to us.

Distribute black poster board, one piece per family. Distribute the rest of the supplies evenly between the groups. Give each family a copy of the "God's Promise Poster" instructions (p. 23) and a copy of the "God, the Promise Keeper" handout (p. 26).

• **What do you remember thinking or feeling as you worked on this "God's Promise Poster"?**

• **How did God keep his promises to Abraham and bless him?**

• **Name some ways God keeps promises to us and blesses us.**

• **For which of God's promises to you are you most grateful?**

Say: As children of the promises given to Abraham, we realize that God is also faithful to us. He kept all of his promises to Abraham, and he keeps all of his promises to us. He has given us dear family members and friends and has blessed us in many other ways. Hold up your "God's Promise Posters" for everyone to enjoy. Have each family share some highlights of its poster with the entire group.

• **Why do you believe having an heir and descendants was so important to Abraham?**

• **For what people in your life are you most grateful? Why?**

Say: As you look at your poster, be reminded of the blessings you have through the promises God keeps, and also through the people he has brought to your life. They represent some of the promises of God. Count your blessings like the sand on the seashore and the stars in the sky. They are very numerous.

COVENANT TIME

Sacrifices and Promises
(up to 3 minutes)

Say: Sometimes God tests us to see if we are willing to sacrifice things that are important to us so that we clearly trust him to come through with his promises for us. Some may have to sacrifice high-paying jobs that keep them away from their families for lower-paying jobs that allow them quality family time—and trust that God will provide for them. Some kids have to leave behind friends who always get them into trouble and trust God to provide them with friends who will bring out their best. Ask:

• **In what ways has God kept his promises to your family?**

• **How has God blessed your family?**

• **What might God be asking you to sacrifice today so he can**

FOR Older KIDS

Encourage families to allow older children to take the lead in designing the "God's Promise Poster" in the Family Learning Activity. They will enjoy this creative responsibility.

provide you with something better?

• How might God be nudging you to trust him more in some area of your life?

Provide paper and a pen to each family. Families should separately discuss the following questions:

• What might God want us to sacrifice (give back) to him?

• What might we need to rid from our home life to draw closer to God as a family?

Say: **Write a few sentences telling God what your family is going to do. Have each family member sign the covenant.** After about five minutes, lead the group in praying a prayer of thanksgiving to God for keeping his promises and for increasing our faith so that we learn to trust and obey him. Thank him that though we will sometimes have to make difficult decisions and sacrifices, the blessings of being an obedient child of God are great. Families should pray within their family groups according to what each shared in the discussion above. Close with each family asking God for help in keeping the promises made during Covenant Time.

OPTIONAL SNACK TIME

Serve star-shaped cookies, finger sandwiches, or finger gelatin. The stars are a reminder of the promise made to Abraham. They also remind us of God's hands of provision, his faithfulness to us, and the blessings he has given to our families.

Definitions

Faith . . . . Wholehearted and steady belief

Trust . . . . Assured reliance on some person or thing

Obey . . . . To do as directed or asked; to comply

Promise . . . A declaration that one will do or refrain from doing something specified

Sacrifice . . To offer, suffer loss of, give up

Making a "God's Promise Poster"

Work with your family to create a "God's Promise Poster" as a reminder that God is a Promise Keeper and is faithful to all of his promises. Follow these directions to make your poster.

1. Spread glue on the bottom of the poster, and sprinkle with sand. Shake off the excess sand. This will remind you of the sand of the seashore.

2. Use glue and blue cellophane to represent the sea. Put it above the sand.

3. On the rest of the black poster board, place gold, silver, and fluorescent star stickers of various sizes. As each family member places a star, he or she should name a promise God has kept or name a person who is a blessing. Family members can write these promises in one or two words and the names of the people they mention using a glow-in-the-dark pen. If you run out of stars, have families use white or fluorescent yellow chalk to draw stars on the black poster board.

4. Next, glue on the Bible verses from the "God, the Promise Keeper" handout (p. 26) wherever there is room on the poster, on the front or back. Using the chalk or marker, write other promise verses from the Bible on your poster. Spend approximately fifteen minutes on this project.

God's Faithfulness
THE PROMISED SON
Genesis 21:1-8

When God told seventy-five-year-old Abram and his wife Sarai that he would bless Abram and make him a great nation, the couple had no children (Genesis 12). But Abram believed God. Ten years passed and Sarai and Abraham just got older and older and maybe just a little bit slower. Sarai was still childless, but God said that Abram's heir would come from his own body, even though he was now eighty-five years old (Genesis 15). When Abram was ninety-nine years old, God told him that Sarah would give birth to a son the following year (Genesis 17). Sarah laughed in amazement because she was very old, beyond childbearing years. One year later, she laughed again, this time with joy as she gave birth to a son named Isaac, a name that means "He laughs." After twenty-five years of trusting and waiting, Abraham (his new name, given to him in Genesis 17:5) and Sarah held in their arms their precious baby son, the heir through whom countless descendants would be born. The promised son had finally arrived.

Have one or two family members share answers to the following questions:

• **Tell of a promise someone made to you (no names necessary) that they took much longer to follow through on than you expected.**

• **How did you feel? Why?**

Read Genesis 21:1-8 aloud in your family group. Then discuss these questions:

• **How might Abraham and Sarah have felt as you did?**

• **How must Sarah and Abraham have felt when Isaac was born?**

Abraham—
GOD'S UNWAVERING, FAITHFUL SERVANT
Genesis 22:1-10

In Genesis 22, God commanded Abraham to do something difficult beyond comprehension. Though God had said, "It is through Isaac that your offspring will be reckoned" (Hebrews 11:18), he tested Abraham by saying, "Take your son, your only son, Isaac, whom you love, and go to the region of Moriah. Sacrifice him there as a burnt offering on one of the mountains I will tell you about" (Genesis 22:2). Abraham, some servants, and his son, Isaac, left the next day to make the sacrifice. When he reached the place God had told him to make the sacrifice, Abraham said to the servants, "Stay here with the donkey while I and the boy go over there. We will worship and then we will come back to you" (Genesis 22:5). Even here Abraham had faith that Isaac would somehow be spared. When Abraham reached the spot, he built an altar, arranged the wood on it, bound Isaac, and laid him on the altar. He reached for his knife to slay his son.

Read Genesis 22:1-10 aloud in your family groups, and then discuss these questions:

• **What do you think Abraham was thinking and feeling during this whole trial?**

• **How do you think Abraham could trust God in this situation—without fully understanding why God commanded him to sacrifice his son?**

Read Hebrews 11:17-19.

• **As to your faith and trust in God, how are you most like Abraham? least like Abraham?**

God,
THE UNWAVERING PROMISE KEEPER

Genesis 22:11-18

In Genesis 22:10, Abraham in faith stretched out his hand and took the knife to kill his only son, Isaac. He had waited twenty-five years to receive this son. He had raised the boy to adolescence. This was the one God had promised to give him, the one through whom God promised to bring Abraham descendants that would outnumber the stars in the sky (Genesis 15:5). Why was Abraham willing to obey God by killing this promised son? Because he believed that God's promises were true. He didn't know *how* God would keep his promise, but he knew that God was true to his Word. Perhaps God would raise Isaac from the dead. Abraham did not know what God would do, but he trusted him completely by obeying him fully. Suddenly the angel of the Lord called out to him from heaven. "Abraham! Abraham... Do not lay a hand on the boy," he said. "Do not do anything to him. Now I know that you fear God, because you have not withheld from me your son, your only son." Abraham was given the supreme test of faith, and he trusted God and had faith in him.

Read Genesis 22:11-18, and discuss these questions:

• How did God make what Abraham said in Genesis 22:8 come to pass?

• As a result of Abraham's faithful obedience, what did God promise in Genesis 22:17-18?

25

GOD, THE PROMISE KEEPER

Here is God's promise to Abraham: "I will surely bless you and make your descendants as numerous as the stars in the sky and as the sand on the seashore" (Genesis 22:17).

We are heirs of the promise: "The Lord is faithful to all his promises and loving toward all he has made" (Psalm 145:13).

"Let us hold unswervingly to the hope we profess, for he who promised is faithful" (Hebrews 10:23).

The Fighting Twins
Jacob and Esau

LESSON FOCUS:

Family members show respect for each other when they are honest and fair.

TEXT:
Genesis 25; 27;
Proverbs 6:16-19

OBJECTIVES:

Family members will
- experience a temptation to be dishonest and respond with honesty or dishonesty,
- explore the story of Jacob and Rebekah's deception of Isaac and Esau to see the harm cheating and dishonesty can bring,
- discuss ways to be more truthful and fair with one another, and
- commit to honesty and fairness in the family (and beyond).

STUFF YOU WILL NEED:

Name tags; pencils; paper; bathroom tissue; smelly stuff in a sack (such as a sliced lemon, a Jolly Rancher candy, pine needles, spices, a dirty sock, a doughnut or cookie, and some perfume or cologne); chalk and a chalkboard, copies of the "Expensive Soup" script (p. 35), a board game for each family (Sorry!, Chutes and Ladders, Candyland, Monopoly, The Game of Life), and a "Family Covenant" worksheet (p. 36) for each family.

GATHERING ACTIVITY

Mind Game

Everyone will be together for this opening activity and discussion. As families arrive, distribute paper and pencils, keeping one of each for yourself.

Say: **Hey, let's start today with a little pop quiz!** After the groans, continue. **Actually we won't do a pop quiz, but we will play a mind game. Anybody here like mind games?** Pause. **Anybody you know like mind games?** Pause. **Well, either way, you'll like this one. Here we go!**

Begin by having people number their papers from one to ten down the left margin since they will be playing ten rounds. Let them know that the winner, the person with the highest score, will win a "brain food" special treat (candy). To play, think of a number between one and ten, and write it on your paper. Then have people individually guess what number you have written and write it on their papers. After everyone has guessed, let them know what number you wrote down. They each should then score themselves in a column to the right of the guess. (It is very important to have them score themselves each round.) If the person guessed the right number, he or she gets ten points; within two of the right number, five points; if the player misses by more than four, he or she loses five points.

Play ten rounds. Don't hesitate to use the same number more than once, especially toward the end, when everyone assumes you'll probably just use each number once. After ten rounds, determine a winner, and award the person with the "brain food."

Say: **Now let's look into an interesting point. Tear off a little piece of your paper, and write either "no" or "yes" to the following question: Did you cheat during this game? (For example, did you erase a number, and then write in the correct one after you knew it; or did you pretend you guessed correctly when you didn't?) No one will know. Your response will be totally confidential.**

Collect these pieces of paper (preserving anonymity). Tally the votes, and let everyone know the tally. Ask:

• **How did you feel during this game, especially as it became clear others had more points than you did?**

If anyone cheated, use the statement below and the questions that follow. Otherwise, skip the next two questions.

• **This was just a guessing game that required no skill; the only prize was a candy bar. So why do you think some of us cheated?**

• **In what way is cheating, even in a game like this, a big deal?** Pick up here if no one cheated.

• **In this game, what might have made it tempting to cheat?**

• **What kept you from cheating?**

• **How is honesty important in this game? After all it's just a game.**

• **Is honesty the best policy, as the old saying goes? Why?**

• **Why is honesty important to God? Why should it be important to us?**

Say: **It seems like many people fail to see how honesty in all things really matters. Some feel that it's OK to be a little fast and loose with the truth as long as nobody seems to get hurt. But I think many of you are like me: You value honesty and realize dishonesty always hurts somebody. Let's look a little bit more closely today at how dishonesty caused some pain and harm to a biblical family and why honesty and forgiveness are so important.**

BIBLE STORY TIME

Expensive Soup

(up to 20 minutes)

Write the following focus on the chalkboard: "Family members show respect for each other when they are honest and fair." Say: **This is what we'll talk about today, showing one another respect in our families by being honest and fair. To begin, let's look at the damage that dishonest and unfair acts by a family member can cause harm to others in the family.**

Families should meet together for the skit but discuss the questions that follow within their families. Have family groups read the story of Jacob and Esau in Genesis 25:19-34. After reading the Bible story, have some volunteers from the group act out this part of the lesson story in a skit. You'll need three volunteers—one to be the narrator, one to be Esau, and one to be Jacob. Distribute the scripts (p. 35), and then have the volunteers act out the skit.

Either write the questions below on the chalkboard or provide copies to all families. Family members should discuss the following questions:

• **What do you think about Esau trading his inheritance for a bowl of bean soup?**

• **Why do you think he did this?**

Gain the attention of the whole group, and say: **A birthright belongs to the oldest son. It is a larger share of the inheritance. In other words, the oldest son gets more land, cattle, money, and tents than the other sons.**

Giving away a birthright is like giving away a sports car, a Jet Ski, the best video game system, the newest computer, and a beautiful beach house—all just for a bowl of bean soup! Esau didn't consider his future. He thought only about his hunger. He wanted to eat, and he wanted to eat now!

Scratch 'n' Sniff

(up to 20 minutes)

Say: **Let's look at another example of the harm dishonesty and unfairness can cause in a family.**

All families will participate together in this activity. Provide name tags for all participants. Encourage people to introduce themselves. Tell them it's very important to try to remember each other's names; they will see why later. After a few minutes, begin the activity.

Have family groups read the story of Jacob and Esau in Genesis 27:1-35. After reading the Bible story, each family should have a short discussion. Either write the following questions on the chalkboard or provide copies to all families, and have families discuss them among themselves:

Ask:

• **How was what Jacob and Rebekah did dishonest?**

• **Who was hurt as a result of their deception? How?**

• **How does it feel to be cheated out of something?**

• **How do you think Esau felt after being cheated out of his inheritance?**

• **Cheating certainly makes people feel bad, but why else is cheating wrong?**

Gain the attention of the whole group, and say: **Cheating is taking the shortcut. It's taking something you didn't earn or that doesn't belong to you. Cheating is a form of stealing. We are not to get what we want or get our way by cheating or being tricky. We are to be honest and fair and trust God, even if it's harder to do or even if we don't always get what we want or get our way. Jacob wasn't honest or fair. Instead of relying on God, he tried to rely on his own trickery and hurt his family—and himself—deeply.**

As a result, Isaac blessed Jacob, giving him wealth and power. Esau was furious! Though he kept crying, "Bless me too, my father...bless me too!" there was nothing that could be changed. The damage was done.

To review key points of the story, have fun with the following scratch and sniff activities.

Have all the children line up in a single line, each standing three feet apart. Have them stand beside you, but not near the bag of smelly stuff (keep it hidden).

Say: **Isaac was blind, so Jacob was able to take advantage of him and trick him by pretending to be his brother. Isaac smelled him and touched him to try and determine if it was Jacob or Esau standing before him to receive his blessing. Because Jacob was wearing what his brother would wear, he smelled like his brother, and because he wore animal skins on his arm, he felt hairy like his brother, too. Let's experience a little bit of blindness right now and try to identify things only through smell or touch.**

Blindfold each of the children with bathroom tissue by wrapping the paper around their eyes three or four times and then tying it in the back. Be sure kids can't peek out.

Say: **Pretend you are blind, just like Isaac. We will hold different items under your nose, and you must identify them by smell. Each time I allow you to smell something, I will also let you whisper in my ear what you think it is. If you can, don't say it out loud; whisper your answer in my ear. No peeking!**

Bring out the smelly stuff that you have kept hidden in a sack, and see if kids can guess the items. Bring out the items one at a time and walk down the line, allowing each child in turn to guess. Allow kids three to four minutes for this activity.

Now it's the parents' turn. Blindfold the parents, and have them stand with you.

Say: Pretend you are blind, just like Isaac. He sent his son Esau out to hunt for game to prepare his favorite meal. Isaac told Esau that when he came back, he would give him something. Esau was a rugged and hairy hunter. Isaac, being blind, had to feel his son's face to see if it was hairy Esau or smooth Jacob.

Your job is to feel children's faces and try to identify whose face you are feeling. Try to remember the names of the people you met.

Have children come up to where you and the blindfolded parents are standing. The blindfolded parents can only touch the faces of the children. If necessary, guide their hands towards the chins and necks. After a parent has successfully identified a child, those two can stop playing. Stop the activity after three minutes.

Either write the following questions on the chalkboard or provide copies to families, and have families discuss them.

• How did it feel to have to rely on your senses of smell and touch?

• Do you think Isaac was especially hurt by Jacob's deception? Why?

• What can we learn about honesty and fairness in the family from Jacob's mistakes?

Read Proverbs 6:16-19.

• Why do you think God hates "a lying tongue"? "hands that shed innocent blood"? "a heart that devises wicked schemes"? "feet that are quick to rush into evil"? "a false witness that pours out lies"? "a man who stirs up dissension among brothers" through anger, hatred, or fighting?

Gain everyone's attention, and say: We had fun with this exercise, but the story itself is quite sad. A brother cheats his brother out of the inheritance. The inheritance is the money and things that a parent or grandparent passes on to his son or daughter before he or she dies. Jacob tricked his brother Esau and got his father's blessing and inheritance. He cheated his way into the money, but lost his brother's respect. Remember, family members show respect for each other when they are honest and fair.

FAMILY LEARNING ACTIVITY

Table Game

(up to 25 minutes)

Families will be separate for this activity. Have each family sit at a table together, and give each family a board game.

Say: **We are going to play a board game. You will play by the rules with two exceptions. First, the person whose birthday is closest to today gets a "double blessing." Every time it's that person's turn, he or she gets to have two turns in a row. Second, the person in your group who is wearing the most blue gets only half a turn. That means whatever numbers that person rolls, or whatever points that person receives, are cut in half. Everyone else plays by the regular rules. Play for about ten minutes.** After playing the game the family should have a short discussion. Either write the following questions on the chalkboard or provide copies to all families, and then families should discuss them.

• How is this different from how we usually play the game?

• How did it feel to be the person who received the double blessing?

• How did it feel to be the person who received the half blessing?

• How was this unfair?

Gain everyone's attention, and say: **We already know that cheating can hurt a family, but unfairness can also hurt a family. And the way we played this game was unfair. For family members to be happy together, to get along and not fight, we must try to keep things fair. A good place to start is by being truthful and not cheating.**

Because Isaac and Rebekah each had a "favored" child, things were unfair in the family. It made Jacob and Esau enemies. Rebekah was dishonest, and, no doubt, Jacob picked up on the same sin. Instead of talking to her husband and trusting God for things to work out, Rebekah took things into her own hands and tried to change the situation by her own efforts and tricks. It only led to more problems.

Write the following questions on the chalkboard or provide copies to all families, and then families should discuss them.

• Why is truthfulness important?

• How would you rate our family's level of honesty and fairness: high, average, or low? Why?

• What are some ways we can be more truthful with each other?

Say: We must show respect for each other by being honest and fair. To be dishonest and unfair to others in our family can cause huge problems. Besides, God hates dishonesty and loves honesty, and we all want to please God.

COVENANT TIME

Family Covenant
(up to 5 minutes)

Say: As a family, decide how you will apply this lesson. Record your promise using the "Family Covenant" worksheet (p. 36). Consider ideas such as "We will always play fair," "We will always be honest with one another—even when it's the hardest thing to do," and "We won't cheat each other—not even in little things like taking another cookie (the last one) when we know another family member has not had one." Have family members sign their names, and have a parent add the date. Keep the covenant in a prominent spot as a reminder.

As a family group, pray for each other to be able to learn to stick to the promises made on the covenant. Pray for your family to be truthful, fair, and not tricky.

Note: The "Family Covenant" worksheet (p. 36) can be used with each lesson in this book, if desired.

OPTIONAL SNACK TIME

Serve Twinkies snack cakes, Reese's Peanut Butter Cups, or other goodies that come in "twin packs." Make reference to the twins, Jacob and Esau.

EXPENSIVE SOUP

Narrator: Once upon an old time in a faraway land, there was a mighty hunter named Esau.

Esau: *(Marches out, flexes.)* I am a *mighty hungry man!* Too bad TV dinners aren't invented yet.

Narrator: Once upon an old time nearby was the hunter's brother, famed Chef Jacob.

Jacob: *(In a mock French accent)* You can call me Jacque *(pronounced "Jawck")*, and I am fixing my stew magnifique. Want some?

Narrator: I can't talk with stew in my mouth.

Esau: I am starved from all my hunting and gathering. I want some!

Jacob: Give me your birthright in trade. I want first shot at all of Dad's wealth—the cattle, the money, the whole enchilada.

Esau: What's an *enchilada?*

Jacob: Never mind, you cuisine-challenged sibling.

Esau: Huh?

Jacob: Give me your favored spot with Dad.

Esau: Oh, all right. What good does it do me if I starve to death? It's yours.

Jacob: Swear?

Esau: Yeah, sure. Now where is that delicious stew I am smelling?

Jacob: It's bean soup. Enjoy.

Family Covenant

Lesson Date _____

Lesson Number _____

Lesson Title _____

We Learned:

We Promise To:

Family Member Signatures and Date

_____   _____

_____   _____

_____   _____

Good From Bad

Joseph and His Family

LESSON FOCUS:

God can bring good out of bad situations.

TEXT:
**Genesis 37; 39;
42–50**

OBJECTIVES:

Family members will
• evaluate their beliefs about why bad things happen,
• explore Joseph's trials and see how God used them for good,
• identify ways in which God might work for good through bad situations in their own lives, and
• praise God for his goodness and trust him to use present bad situations in our lives for good.

STUFF YOU WILL NEED:

Bibles, poster board, markers, current newspapers and newsmagazines, scissors, newsprint, pens, "Joseph and His Brothers" script copies (pp. 44-45), and index cards for each family.

GATHERING ACTIVITY

Bad Beliefs?

(up to 10 minutes)

Say: **In this lesson we're going to talk about bad times and what they are good for—if anything. To begin, let's look at some beliefs people have about bad times and why they even happen in the first place.**

To start, everyone should be together and sitting in chairs. You will then read each of the following beliefs in turn, each time encouraging people to indicate their opinion or level of agreement with the belief in one of the following three ways:

Totally true: Stand up on your chair, and give double thumbs up signs.

Somewhat true: Stand up, and hold arms out in front of you, rotating hands by turning palms up and down.

Never true: Stay seated, and give double thumbs down.

As you read the beliefs in the following list, pause to allow everyone to indicate their opinion or level of agreement with the belief. For each belief, ask one or two people to explain their opinions.

Bad Beliefs?

• We can avoid having bad stuff happen in our lives if we love God enough and are committed to him.

• Bad times are just that, bad, not good in any way.

• We have little or no control over the bad stuff we experience.

• Christians have less bad stuff happen in their lives than non-Christians do.

• Bad stuff happens always just to teach us something.

• God uses bad stuff to teach us things because he can't think of a better way to teach us.

• Bad stuff happens equally to good people and bad people.

• Those who experience bad things in their lives do so because of some sin in their life they may not even know of.

• Bad stuff happening in our lives is always a tool Satan uses to discourage us and undermine our faith.

• Bad stuff in our lives can make us either bitter or better.

After reading each belief and allowing a few people to give their opinions after each one, lead a short discussion. Ask:

• **With which belief about bad things did you most agree? most disagree? Why?**

• **What other beliefs have you heard about bad stuff and why it happens in our lives?**

• **What does the last belief I read mean to you: "Bad stuff in our lives can make us either bitter or better"?**

• **How does God use bad stuff for our good?**

Say: **We have a lot of beliefs about bad stuff, why it happens, and how God uses it. But the bad things that happen in our lives are not just bad things that happen. God can take any bad thing that has happened in our lives and "work all things together for our good." Let's look at the story of Joseph and how God worked all things together (good and bad) for his good.**

BIBLE STORY TIME

Joseph and His Brothers
(up to 20 minutes)

Everyone should remain together for a skit.

Before class, cut poster board into 8½ x 11 size or bigger for cue cards that should read: "Hum theme music," "Boo!" "Applaud + cheer," "Hiss," "Shout 'Joseph! Joseph! Joseph!' "

Find nine volunteers to play the parts of Joseph, Joseph's family (one to play Jacob and at least three to play the brothers), Potiphar, Potiphar's wife, Pharaoh, and the cupbearer in the skit. This skit is a no-prep, no-practice-or-props-necessary narrated skit. Actors will simply do what you read as you read it, so actors should know they will just have fun—no work involved except to really ham it up.

Enlist someone to hold up cue cards, and give them a copy of the script. The cue card person should follow along in the script and hold up cue cards when called for in the script. Everyone else who are not actors are to provide sound effects and crowd response as cued by the cue cards.

As you give the following tips to the actors and the cue card person, have the sound effects people choose a theme song to hum as called for in the script. Here are the tips:

Actors

- Really ham it up!
- Do or say whatever is read aloud for your character to do or say.
- When you aren't saying something or doing something, freeze (in a dramatic pose—different every time).

Cue card person

- Keep cue cards spread out next to you on a table (not held in a stack in your hand).
- If people don't perform their sound effect satisfactorily, hold the card up again.
- Throw in extra cues if you feel like it (or make up some of your own cue cards).

Say: **God has the power to change hard and sad situations into something beautiful. Today we're going to talk about one person in the Bible who faced many difficult situations, but God worked through all of those situations for good.**

After the story, have family members discuss these questions, which you should either write on a chalkboard or copy for each family:

- **In what bad situations did Joseph find himself in this story?**
- **How did Joseph respond to the things that happened to him?**
- **Why do you think Joseph was able to respond in this way?**
- **How did God make good things happen through the bad things in Joseph's life?**

After giving families up to five minutes to discuss the skit and the Bible account of Joseph, get the attention of the entire group.

Say: **How much good we gain from bad times often has a lot to do with us and our attitude toward bad times and our faith and trust in God. If we refuse to look for the good that can come from bad situations, we can keep ourselves from seeing the good things and we may begin to harbor bad feelings toward God. That is where our trust in him comes in. We must trust and believe that he is working all things together for our good. This keeps our eyes open to see the good that he is bringing or has brought to us from our bad or sad situation.**

FAMILY LEARNING ACTIVITY

In the News

(up to 15 minutes)

For the first part of this activity, families should sit separately. Give each family several current newspapers and newsmagazines, a pair of scissors, newsprint, and a pen.

Gain the attention of everyone, and say: **As we saw in the Bible story, God can use just about any difficult situation to bring good. Let's see how this might be the case in today's society. I'd like you to look through the newspapers and newsmagazines I've given you. Each family will need to choose one article about a bad situation. For example, you might find an article about a bad thing (perhaps a natural disaster, someone is injured in an accident, or someone is bankrupt after winning the lottery and spending it all). When you've found an article that interests you, cut it out. In your family group, brainstorm ways that God might bring good out of the bad situation in your article. For example, if your article was about a natural disaster, maybe the situation could cause a community to pull together, cause people to care for their neighbors, or perhaps make people even more grateful to God for what he has provided for them. Think of several possibilities for each article, and write them on your newsprint.**

Give families several minutes to do this. Then have each family display and describe its article for the large group, with family members sharing their thoughts about it and how God could bring good even out of the bad. After these presentations, keep the newsprint presentations on display.

Then have family members discuss within their families these questions, which you should either write on the chalkboard or copy for each family:

• **What were you thinking and feeling as you worked on this project?**

• **Was it easy or hard for you to see how God could work for good in these stories? Why?**

• **How does it encourage you to know that God will use even the bad things and the hard times you go through for your good?**

• **How have you seen God work for good in bad things in your life too?**

Gain the attention of the group, and say: **It can be hard to see how God can bring something good out of some genuinely tragic events and happenings. It is just one more way that God is one who can make even the impossible possible. Let's look now at a verse that gives us an incredible promise in this regard.**

COVENANT TIME

Praise and Trust

(up to 10 minutes)

Families should sit separately for this activity. Give each family a Bible, index cards, and a pen. Have families read Romans 8:28a together and discuss what they think the verse means. Then have family members discuss within their family these questions, which you should either write on the chalkboard or copy for each family:

• **What is one bad thing in your life from which you believe God brought good?**

• **How is the good God brought from your bad situation like the good God brought from Joseph's bad situations? How is it different?**

• **How did it make you feel to see God bring good from bad in your life?**

• **How should we respond to God's bringing good from bad in our lives?**

Gain the attention of the group, and say: **There are two responses we should have to the message in Romans 8:28a. The first is a response of praise, and the second is a response of trust. We can praise God because of the good he has brought from bad in the past, both in our lives and in the lives of others. We need to trust God to continue to work through all of the present situations in our lives for good.**

On your index cards, each of you should write on one side the text of Romans 8:28a. On the other side, write a prayer to God praising him for the good things he has brought you in the past from bad things. Then continue the prayer by writing on your card a present bad, sad, or difficult time you are going through and how you are trusting him with it.

Give family members time to each write their prayers to God, and then say: **Now let's close in prayer together. Let's do a popcorn**

FOR Younger KIDS

To help make the "In the News" activity more real for younger kids, have them share about people they know who are in difficult or sad situations. Then brainstorm ways God might work through those situations to bring about good.

prayer. I'll begin the prayer, then each of you can pray within your own family group the prayers you wrote. Then I'll close the prayer.

Pray: Loving Father, we are so thankful that you work for the good in all things for those who love you. We respond to you by... pause for a few minutes to allow families to pray their written prayers, and then close by saying: **Amen.**

OPTIONAL SNACK TIME

Make a batch of "Good From Bad" banana pudding. Add vanilla wafers and well-ripened bananas to banana-flavored pudding made from a mix. By using the well-ripened bananas, you are seeing something good coming from something bad (almost!).

Field-Test FINDINGS

Consider having participants sign up to bring snacks for the class each week. The leader or a designate should call two days in advance of the class or service to remind these families of their commitment to bring the snack and to send a thank you card to the family after the lesson.

FOR Older KIDS

Remember to utilize the resources older kids bring. They can help you distribute supplies, be some of your most willing actors for dramas, and are even able to lead certain activities (like the opening "Bad Beliefs?" activity).

Joseph and His Brothers

Characters:

Joseph, Joseph's family, Potiphar, Potiphar's wife, Pharaoh, cupbearer.

Cue card "cues" are in parentheses and in italics throughout the script: "Hum theme music," "Boo!" "Applaud + cheer," "Hiss," "Shout 'Joseph! Joseph! Joseph!' " "ooOOhh!"

(Cue card "Hum theme music")

Joseph *("Shout 'Joseph! Joseph! Joseph' ")* had eleven brothers. His father, Jacob, loved and hugged all of his sons very much, *("Applaud + cheer")* but he loved Joseph the most, so he hugged him and lifted him up *("Shout 'Joseph! Joseph! Joseph!' ")*. Because he loved Joseph so much, Jacob made him a coat with many beautiful colors *("ooOOhh!")*. Joseph's brothers were mad and jealous and they gnashed their teeth and made angry sounds because they thought that their dad loved Joseph more than he loved them *("Boo!")*. His brothers became even more angry and jealous when Joseph began to have dreams about his brothers in which they were serving him and bowing down to him, especially when he pantomimed them bowing down. All this made the brothers even angrier with Joseph *("Hiss")*. Because they were so angry, the brothers huddled together and decided to kill Joseph *("Boo!" and "hiss")*. But then, one of the brothers got a big idea and decided they shouldn't kill Joseph but just get rid of him. All the brothers agreed and rubbed their hands together wickedly. They sold Joseph into slavery, and he was bound and led away *("Boo!" and "Hiss")*.

The traders to whom Joseph was sold were on their way to Egypt, far away from Joseph's home in Israel. When the traders got to Egypt, they sold Joseph to an Egyptian man named Potiphar. Joseph became one of Potiphar's trusted servants; sometimes he even had Joseph carry him on his back *("Hum theme music")*. Joseph rose to a high position in Potiphar's household *("Shout 'Joseph! Joseph! Joseph!' " and "Applaud + cheer")*.

Then one day, Potiphar's wife took hold of Joseph and tried to get Joseph to do something bad *("Boo!")*, something that was a sin against God *("Hiss")*. But Joseph loved God and wouldn't sin against God *("Applaud + cheer")*. Potiphar's wife was angry with Joseph, so she threw a temper tantrum. When she couldn't get Joseph to sin, she lied and accused Joseph of attacking her *("Boo!" and "hiss")*.

After Joseph was falsely accused, he was thrown into jail even though he had done nothing wrong *("Boo!" and "hiss")*. While Joseph was in jail, Pharaoh threw his baker and his cupbearer into jail just because he was angry with them *("Boo!")*.

While they were in jail, both of these men had strange dreams that had them tossing, turning, and doing handstands as they lay in bed. Joseph was able, with God's help, to tell them both what their dreams meant *("Shout 'Joseph! Joseph! Joseph!' ")*.

Joseph told the baker that his dream meant that the Pharaoh would kill him *("Boo!")*, and he told the cupbearer that his dream meant that he would get his job with the Pharaoh back *("Applaud + cheer")*. Joseph made sure that both men understood that he was only able to interpret their dreams because God helped him *("Applaud + cheer")*.

Joseph asked the cupbearer to remember him and to tell the Pharaoh about him when he was released from jail. But the cupbearer forgot all about him *("Boo!")*.

One night, the Pharaoh lay in bed tossing and turning with some wild dreams. No one could help him understand the dreams *("Boo!")*. Then the cupbearer remembered Joseph and the amazing gift God had given him *("Applaud + cheer")*! He told the Pharaoh all about Joseph, and the Pharaoh asked Joseph to come and help him understand his dreams *("Shout 'Joseph! Joseph! Joseph!' ")*.

The Pharaoh told Joseph about his dreams. One dream was about seven skinny cows eating seven fat cows. Another dream was about seven skinny heads of grain eating seven really big heads of grain. The Pharaoh asked Joseph what he thought the dreams were about. God *("Applaud + cheer")* told Joseph what to tell the Pharaoh: The seven big cows and seven big heads of grain meant that there would be seven years of lots of food, and the seven skinny cows and seven skinny heads of grain meant that there would be seven years of no food *("ooOOhh!")*. Joseph told the Pharaoh that he should put someone in charge of all the food so that some food could be saved during the seven good years *("ooOOhh!")*. Then the people would have food during the seven bad years

("Applaud + cheer").

The Pharaoh put Joseph in charge of the entire food gathering! Now he was one of the most powerful men in all of Egypt *("Applaud + cheer")*! Joseph went from being in jail to being in charge of important things *("Shout 'Joseph! Joseph! Joseph!' ")*. God is the one who helped him *("Applaud + cheer")*.

When the seven bad years came, there was no food in Israel, where Joseph's father and brothers lived *("Boo!")*. Joseph's father, Jacob, sent his sons stumbling and tripping over themselves all the way to Egypt because they had heard there was food there.

The brothers came and bowed down before Joseph—just like the dream Joseph had when he was a boy! The brothers didn't recognize Joseph, however; they were just coming to buy food. But Joseph recognized his brothers. He felt sorry for them. He didn't hate them *("Applaud + cheer")*. He still loved them, even though they had been so cruel to him *("Shout 'Joseph! Joseph! Joseph!' ")*.

Joseph finally broke down weeping and told his brothers who he was. They couldn't believe it. Joseph told them he forgave them, and he went on to tell them that even though they did evil things, God used those things for good in his life and other people's lives *("Applaud + cheer")*.

Even though bad things happened to Joseph, he still trusted God and forgave those who hurt him *("Shout 'Joseph! Joseph! Joseph!' ")*. God gave him the strength to do this *("Applaud + cheer" and "Hum theme music")*.

45

Show Me the Way
Moses

LESSON

5

LESSON FOCUS:

God guides and protects his people.

OBJECTIVES:

Family members will
- realize just how dramatically God protected Moses;
- explore through drama some key times in Moses' life as found in Exodus 2–3;
- discuss various ways in which God offers us his protection and guidance;
- offer thanks to God for his guidance and protection and petition him to provide guidance and protection in specific areas of each family member's life.

STUFF YOU WILL NEED:

2x2-foot squares of cardboard; baby doll in a basket; masking tape; permanent markers in different colors; simple Bible costumes to act out scenes from the story of Moses (optional); a life preserver (or a cardboard cutout of one), a blanket, a seat belt (or a picture of one), an umbrella, a compass, and other items that represent protection and guidance; paper; pens; and a "God Protects and Leads Moses" handout (pp. 54-56), and a small flashlight for each family.

TEXT:
Exodus 2–3

Field-Test FINDINGS

Consider two different kinds of promotions for these *Family Sunday School Fun* lessons in your church advertising or bulletin. Target adults and kids separately so it doesn't seem like a "thing for kids" to parents or a "thing for adults" to kids.

GATHERING ACTIVITY

River Crossing Rescue

(up to 15 minutes)

Gather everyone together for this activity.

Before class, use masking tape to mark the sides of the "river," approximately twenty feet in width. Put 2x2-foot cardboard squares on the floor in the "river," placing them the way that steppingstones would be placed for someone to step on while attempting a river crossing (at least 1½ feet apart).

Say: **The space between the masking tape lines is a large, crocodile-infested river! Every one of you must cross this river—but not just you. This baby will also need to get across safely. You all will line up and cross, and the last person in line will be the official carrier of the baby basket. You are to cross by walking in a single-file line on the steppingstones (cardboard squares). Anyone who accidentally steps into the "water" will be devoured by a vicious crocodile and thus will be out of the game. Oh, just a few little things to keep in mind:**

1) You have only two minutes to get everyone, including the baby, across. (Allow up to ten seconds per person. If you have a large group, have several river crossings.)

2) You cannot move steppingstones.

3) After a steppingstone has been stepped on, it must be touched constantly from then on. If someone isn't touching it in some way—even for an instant—we will ask everyone to freeze, and crocodiles will come and remove the steppingstone. Time will stop as we remove steppingstones.

As many people as necessary (or possible!) may stand on a steppingstone at one time as long as each person has both of his or her feet on the steppingstone. As everyone progresses across the river, anyone who has fallen in (and any unfortunate crocodile "victims") can act as the crocodiles, catching people who fall off the steppingstones and removing the steppingstones when they are vacant.

Allow the group to play the game, and then ask:

• **What was it like to help get this baby across a crocodile-filled river?**

• **What were some of your ideas for protecting the baby and keeping the baby moving?**

• Is protecting this baby like protecting a real baby? Why or why not?

• How do you think the ways you would protect this baby are like the ways God protects you?

Say: Your protection of a baby in that daring crossing of a crocodile-infested river is a fun way to begin looking at a wonderful story in the Bible about someone who was chosen by God to be a great leader. When he was a little baby, God protected this boy in a very miraculous way. His story is found in the book of Exodus. Can anyone guess the name of the person I am talking about?

Give families a few seconds to guess, and then say: It's Moses. Today we're going to learn more about Moses.

BIBLE STORY TIME

God Protects and Leads Moses (up to 20 minutes)

Families will be together for this activity.

Before this activity, lay out Bible costumes if you have them.

Say: **I'd like families to join together to form three larger groups.** (Assign each family group to group 1, 2, or 3; try to keep the large groups relatively even in number.) **Each group will act out one scene. Together, these scenes will form a three-act play called "God Protects and Leads Moses."**

Give each group a "God Protects and Leads Moses" handout (pp. 54-56), and say: **I'll give you a few minutes to prepare your act. To begin, you'll need to select actors to play each of the characters listed. As the Narrator reads through the act, the rest of the characters will pantomime, or act out, what they think their characters would be doing. When the Narrator pauses, the character who the Narrator was speaking about last will say what the character might have said. In a few minutes, each group will present its act to the other groups.**

If you've gathered Bible costumes, give them to families now.

Give groups several minutes to read through and prepare their acts. Then have each group present its act to the other two groups in order. After the third act, lead the whole group in applause. Ask:

• **How did God protect and guide Moses in this story? Explain.**

• What does this story tell us about how God felt about Moses?

• How do you think God feels about you?

• How does God protect and guide you? Explain.

Say: **God cares about each of us just as much as he cares about Moses. That's a great thing about God—he doesn't play favorites. Just as he had a mission and purpose for Moses to live out, so he has a mission and purpose for each of our lives. Just as he protected Moses from those who wanted to kill him, he will protect us and watch over us.**

FAMILY LEARNING ACTIVITY

God's Protective Ways
(up to 15 minutes)

Before this activity, set out the life preserver, the blanket, the seat belt, the umbrella, the compass, one of the flashlights, and any other protective or guiding items you've found where everyone can see them. (If you cannot gather these items, consider drawing them on paper and copying them for family members.) Though all families will have access to these items, families will meet separately for this activity. Distribute paper and pens to family members.

Say: **God protects and guides us in many different ways in our lives, just as he protected and guided Moses. I'd like you, in your family groups, to think about some of the ways that God protects each of you. Here's how: First, I'd like you as a family to choose one of the protective items I have displayed here. Don't take it; just note the one you've chosen. Once you've chosen your item, take a few moments to write down on your paper all the ways you might use that item for protection or guidance in your everyday lives. Do that now.**

Give family groups a few minutes to do this, and then say: **Now I'd like you to think of one way that your item reminds you of God's guidance or protection. For example, if you've chosen the flashlight, you might say, "The flashlight is like God's protection and guidance because it helps us know where we're going in the dark, and it keeps us from tripping over things that might hurt us."**

Give families a few moments to do this.

Ask:

• How did God protect and guide Moses in the way you discussed?

• How is God's guidance and protection like the item you discussed? How is it different?

• Can you think of a time God protected and guided you in this way? Explain.

Say: Now I'd like families, one at a time, to come up to the front. When you're here, you'll show us the item you've chosen, tell us all of the ways the item might protect and guide you in your everyday lives, and tell how the item might show God's guidance and protection. Try to get each family member involved in your demonstration in some way.

Allow families five minutes to prepare. Start with one family, and continue until every family has had a chance to demonstrate its item.

Ask:

• How do you think Moses must have felt to have God's protection and guidance?

• How does it feel to you to have God's protection and guidance?

• Think of a time you knew God was protecting you. What happened? How did you feel?

• What can you do when you feel you need God's protection and guidance?

Say: In our story today, God kept Moses safe from Pharaoh and then even made him a member of the royal family. He allowed Moses to be adopted as the son of a princess. The years in Pharaoh's court prepared Moses for the plans that God had for him and for the nation of Israel in the future. God chose Moses to be the leader of his people. God works in amazing ways to protect and guide his people to serve him.

COVENANT TIME

God Protects and Leads Our Family (up to 15 minutes)

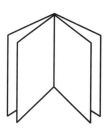

Before this activity, use the diagram in the margin as a guide for creating your own journal.

Give each family two sheets of paper and some colorful markers.

FOR Younger KIDS

Younger family members may have a difficult time creating and understanding abstract analogies for God's protection and guidance. If so, you may want to provide old magazines, scissors, glue sticks, and construction paper and have families create "Protection and Guidance" collages. Families will search for pictures that somehow demonstrate protection and guidance, and they will glue them to their papers. Afterward, discuss how God might do the things shown in the pictures.

FOR Older KIDS

Heavily involve older kids in roles for the "God Protects and Leads Moses" skit. They will enjoy expending a little energy and hamming it up.

Say: I'd like to challenge you, as a family, to keep a "God's Guidance and Protection" journal during the coming week. To begin, I'd like you to fold your sheets of paper into a small "book."

Lead families through the steps of folding a journal.

Say: Now, beginning on the first inside page, write the days of the week, one page per day, starting with today. When you've done that, take a few minutes to decorate your journals, especially the "cover." Be sure to write "God's Guidance and Protection Journal" on the cover.

Give families a few minutes to do this, and then say: Now turn to today's page. I'd like you to brainstorm with your family members about all of the things that happened to you today, either individually or as a whole family, that demonstrated God's guidance and protection in your lives. For example, maybe you nearly got hit by another car on your way here, but you escaped uninjured. Write everything you think of on that page.

Give families a minute to do this, and then say: In a moment, we're going to share a prayer to thank God for all of the ways he protected and guided us today. But first, I'd like to tell you how to use these journals during the coming week. In the morning each day, maybe at the breakfast table, I'd like you to share things you think might be happening that day for which you may need God's protection and guidance. For example, maybe you have a big test on that day, or maybe you're having some problems with someone at work. Write a short prayer about those things at the top of the page for that day. Then, in the evening, get back together and share all of the ways God protected and guided you during the day, and write a brief prayer thanking God for his help.

Give each family a flashlight, and ask them to turn their flashlights on. Then turn off the room lights (you may want to close any blinds or curtains as well, so you can make the room as dark as possible).

Say: These flashlights remind us that God is always with us, guiding and protecting us, even when things may seem kind of dark and confusing. I'd like you to share a prayer together in your family now. In a moment, I'll begin the prayer. Then I'd like you to pass the flashlight from one family member to the next. When you're holding the flashlight, I want you thank God for how he has protected you today. Then pray and ask him for guidance or protection in any area of life in which you need them. When everyone is finished, I'll close the prayer.

Start the prayer by saying: **Heavenly Father, thank you so much for constantly guiding our steps and protecting us throughout our lives. We thank you especially for...**

Give families a few minutes to respond, and then close the prayer by saying: **In Jesus' name, amen.**

OPTIONAL SNACK TIME

Serve treats to remind everyone of crocodile eggs. For example, you might serve deviled eggs, hard-boiled eggs, finger-sized egg-salad sandwiches, candy eggs, or marshmallow eggs.

God Protects and Leads Moses

Act 1

Characters:
Narrator
Moses' mother
Moses' father
The princess (Pharaoh's daughter)
Miriam (Moses' sister)
Pharaoh
Moses (use the baby doll in a basket from the "River Crossing Rescue" activity)

*(As the **Narrator** reads the script, he or she should pause for actors to dramatize the events. Actors should say what they think the characters would have said in each situation.)*

Narrator: Many years ago, **Pharaoh**, the leader of Egypt, took all the people of Israel and made them slaves. When he noticed that these Hebrews were strong and rapidly growing in numbers, he ordered that their sons be killed at birth. But the midwives who helped the women give birth feared God more than the king, so they refused to kill the babies. As a result, **Pharaoh** commanded that all his people throw every Jewish baby son into the Nile River. (Pause.)

During this terrifying time, **Moses' mother** gave birth to a son. He was a beautiful baby. For three months, **Moses' mother and father** hid him from the Egyptians. After awhile, **Moses' mother** realized that she could no longer hide her baby. She trusted God to give her a new plan. First, **Moses' mother** made a basket waterproof by covering it with tar. (Pause.)

Then she wrapped a warm blanket around **Moses**, put him into the basket, and carried the basket to the river. She placed the basket in the river where there were lots of reeds. Then she instructed her daughter, **Miriam**, to keep watch over the basket. (Pause.)

Later, **the princess** came down to the river to bathe. She heard baby **Moses** crying and picked him up. She felt sorry for the beautiful little boy. (Pause.)

When **Miriam** saw **the princess** holding the baby, she ran up to talk to her. **Miriam** told her that she knew a woman who could nurse the baby and take care of him for a while. (Pause.)

The princess named the baby **Moses**, which means, "to draw out of the water," and hired **Moses' mother**, the woman suggested by **Miriam**, to nurse the baby. She didn't know that the woman was actually the baby's real mother! (Pause.)

How happy **Moses' mother** must have been to receive back her baby for a time! (Pause.)

Act 2

Characters:
Narrator
Moses
The princess
Egyptian teacher
Egyptian taskmaster
Hebrew slave
Two Hebrews
Pharaoh

*(As the **Narrator** reads the script, he or she should pause for actors to dramatize the events. Actors should say what they think the characters would have said in each situation.)*

Narrator: When **Moses** was old enough, **the princess** adopted him as her son and took him to the palace to live. (Pause.)

Moses lived at the Pharaoh's palace until he was a grown man. An Egyptian teacher taught him. He had a luxurious life with good food to eat and handsome clothes to wear. Still, God helped him remember his other family. **Moses** knew that he was really a Hebrew, not an Egyptian. (Pause.)

One day, when **Moses** was a man, he saw an **Egyptian taskmaster** beating a **Hebrew slave**. He defended the slave by killing the **Egyptian taskmaster** and burying him in the sand. He had seen the slavery of his people, and it upset him. (Pause.)

Later, he saw **two Hebrews** fighting with each other and tried to stop them. But the Hebrews wouldn't listen to him because they knew that he had killed the Egyptian taskmaster. One of them said, "Who made you ruler and judge over us? Are you thinking of killing me as you killed the Egyptian?" (Pause.)

Pharaoh found out about this matter and tried to kill **Moses**. **Moses** fled to the land of Midian.

Act 3

Characters:
Narrator
Moses
Zipporah (Moses' wife)
Jethro (Moses' father-in-law)
The angel of the Lord

*(As the **Narrator** reads the script, he or she should pause for actors to dramatize the events. Actors should say what they think the character would have said in each situation.)*

Narrator: **Moses** lived in the land of Midian with his wife, **Zipporah**, and their son. He worked for his father-in-law, **Jethro**, tending his flock of sheep. (Pause.)

One day, while **Moses** was herding **Jethro's** sheep, **Moses** came to Mount Horeb. (Pause.)

The angel of the Lord appeared to **Moses** in the middle of a bush that was blazing with fire. The bush wasn't burning up, however. **Moses** looked at the bush and wondered why it didn't burn up. (Pause.)

While **Moses** was looking at the bush, God called out to him, "Moses, Moses." **Moses** replied, "Here I am." God told him, "Do not come any closer. Take off your sandals, for the place where you are standing is holy ground." He also said, "I am the God of your father, the God of Abraham, the God of Isaac and the God of Jacob." (Pause.)

When **Moses** realized that it was really God speaking to him, he was afraid and hid his face. God told him that he had seen the suffering of his people in Egypt and that he would deliver them out of bondage to a land flowing with milk and honey. The land was called Canaan. God also said that he had chosen Moses to go to Pharaoh to tell him to let the people go. (Pause.)

God convinced **Moses** that he would be with him and would help him every step of the way.

Faithful Love

Ruth, Naomi, and Boaz

TEXT:
Ruth 1–4

LESSON FOCUS:

We have a responsibility to faithfully love others, especially family members.

OBJECTIVES:

Family members will

- discover fun and creative ways to show love and kindness to others,
- explore the way Ruth's faithful love and kindess toward Naomi was honored and rewarded by God,
- learn how faithfulness and kindness helped Naomi and Ruth become a solid blended family,
- make smoothies and talk about how every family is a blended family in some respects, and
- discuss how faithfulness and kindness can help them solve family problems.

STUFF YOU WILL NEED:

Two blenders; several large paper bags; items for the "Bag O' Love!" activity (such as an apple, a hand towel, a small pillow, a massage device, lotion, and a snack item that can serve six); chalk and a chalkboard; and, for each family, a Bible, a "Story of Ruth" handout (pp. 63-64), several cans of frozen orange juice concentrate, ice, bananas, strawberries, plastic cups, straws, a "Commitment to Kindness, Faithfulness, and Respect" handout (p. 65), and a pen.

Field-Test FINDINGS

Although these lessons are designed for kids from the first through sixth grades and their parents, some field testers found success by focusing on kids in a three-grade block and their parents. For example, some had kids in first through third grades participating with their parents, and then they had kids in fourth through sixth grades participating with their parents at a later time.

GATHERING ACTIVITY

Bag O' Love!

(up to 15 minutes)

Before class, place items you've gathered for this activity into paper bags, six per bag.

As group members arrive, have them form groups of six people each—no more than six. Give a bag you prepared before class to each group.

Say: **Let's try out a few ways of treating each other with a little bit of love and kindness. Pass the bag around your circle. When it comes to you, quickly pull one item out of the bag without looking. Let's do that first.**

After the bags have been passed and everyone has one item, say: **Now we're going to go around the circle again. When it's your turn, you'll need to use your item to express love or show kindness in some way to a neighbor on either side of you. Sounds easy enough, huh? Well, let's try a round of it and see how it works.** Give groups a minute or so for each member to select an item and use the item to express love or show kindness to a neighbor in some way.

Have groups play five more rounds of this. There is only one catch. For each round, for any one item, group members cannot repeat a way to use the item to show love and kindness. For example, if someone offers a bite of an apple to a neighbor, no one else who chooses the apple in subsequent rounds can use that kindness idea for the apple. When groups have completed six rounds and have placed all the items back in the bags, ask:

• **How did it feel to experience so much kindness?**

• **In your day-to-day life, do you typically experience love and kindness from others or a lack of love and kindness from others? Explain.**

• **Was it easy or hard for you to come up with ideas to express love and kindness? Why?**

• **Why do you think most of us are not more faithfully loving and kind to others?**

Say: **I bet you are all a bit like me, at least in my desire to be more faithfully loving and kind to others, especially to those in my family. Today we're going to examine ways we can treat others with kindness. We're going to do that by looking at the lives of** some biblical people who were known for their love and kindness—Ruth, Naomi, and Boaz. As we look at their story, let's allow ourselves to be challenged by their love and kindness.

BIBLE STORY TIME

The Story of Ruth   (up to 15 minutes)

Families should sit in circles, separate from one another, for this study activity. Distribute to each family a "Story of Ruth" handout (pp. 63-64) and a Bible.

Gain the attention of everyone and say: **You showed love and kindness to others during the last activity. Faithful love and kindness are great ways to show others respect and are great ways to build strong family relationships and friendships. Let's learn more about the importance of kindness in family relationships by looking at one rather unusual family in the Bible.**

Family members should take turns reading the story of Ruth and her family from the "Story of Ruth" handout. There are several places on the handout where they are to stop to either read Bible passages or discuss questions together.

After families have read and discussed their handouts, have them discuss within their own families the questions below. Either write the following questions on the chalkboard or copy them for each family:

• **In what ways did the members of this family treat each other with faithful love and kindness?**

• **Why was it important for these family members to treat one another this way?**

• **What can our family learn from this family about kindness? love? respect?**

Say: **The whole Bible account of Ruth, Naomi, and Boaz is quite remarkable. And although their situation was peculiar, the lesson we can learn from them is unmistakable. Kindness is a non-negotiable key to expressing love and respect to others in our family.**

FAMILY LEARNING ACTIVITY

Smooth Blending

(up to 10 minutes)

Everyone should sit with their families for this activity.

Before this activity, set out at least two electric blenders, several cans of frozen orange juice concentrate, ice, strawberries, bananas, plastic cups, and straws. Make sure each blender can be plugged in to an electric outlet.

Do the following as a teaching demonstration.

Say: **As we saw in the story, God wants us to treat all members of our families with faithful love and kindness, even if we're in difficult situations. Today we're going to exercise our faithful love and kindness by making smoothies for one another. But first I would like to use the making of a smoothie as a demonstration of a point.**

Put one container of frozen orange juice and ice into a blender. Blend it for ten seconds. Give several people a small taste. Ask the people:

• **What does the mixture taste like?**

Say: **Now, I'll add one banana.**

Blend for another ten seconds, and give several people a little taste. Ask:

• **Can you still taste the orange? Can you taste the banana?**

Say: **Now I'll add five strawberries and blend it together.**

Blend for another ten seconds, and give several people a little taste.

Say: **This makes a whole new delicious flavor, doesn't it? We can still taste the orange, banana, and strawberry, but blended together, we get a scrumptious new treat. If we added raspberries, mango, or other fruit, the blend would taste different with each new addition.** Lead a short discussion with everyone in the group. Ask:

• **How are our family members like the different fruits used in this smoothie?**

• **How can treating each other with kindness and faithfulness help all family members to blend together smoothly and be a treat for others as well as ourselves?**

• **In the same way that his smoothie is a sweet treat for us, how might our family be a sweet treat for God when we faithfully love and show kindness to one another?**

• **What are some ways to show faithful love and kindness to other family members?**

FOR Younger KIDS

You may need to help younger kids come up with ways they can use the objects to demonstrate love and kindness to members of their families. If you'd like, you can have younger kids demonstrate various ways they can show love and kindness.

• Tell of a time when someone in your family was especially faithful in their love or kindness to you. How did you feel when they did this?

• In what ways could you be even more faithfully loving and kind to other family members?

• If you were even more faithful in expressing love and kindness to others in the family, how might it change your family?

• When is it especially important to show kindness and faithfulness to the members of your family?

Use the two blenders to make smoothies for everyone.

Say: Ruth's family was a blended family. Ruth was a Gentile, and her husband was a Jew. They came from different backgrounds, religions, and cultures. When Ruth's husband died, she went to live with her mother-in-law, Naomi. She accepted Naomi's God, the God of Israel, as her God. When she married Boaz, the family blended together new personalities, habits, and ideas. Through God's faithfulness and the family members' kindness and faithfulness to each other, this family blended and became a wonderful godly family, concluding many generations later with the birth of the King of Kings, our Lord Jesus.

Every family is like a smoothie. In fact, every family is a blended family. When a man and woman marry, they blend together their lives. Each person brings to the family his or her own personality, tastes, interests, cultural and religious background, ideas, habits, and education. When children are born, each one blends into the mixture and adds a new flavor.

The different personalities and traits of each family member affect the blend. If family members strive to treat each other with kindness and faithfulness, it will make the family blend into the most wonderful smoothie possible. But a rotten lack of love or sour attitudes can really ruin the family flavor. We must maintain the sweet family flavor by going out of our way to faithfully love and show kindness to each other.

Older kids may not grasp all the details about Ruth marrying Boaz and the significance of it, but they will latch on to the whole theme from the story of the importance of faithful love and kindness.

Appoint older kids as judges in each group of six for the opening "Bag O' Love!" activity with the job of determining if someone's idea for how to use an item to express faithful love and kindness is original or a duplicate. They will get a kick out if this.

Older kids are at the age where their faith can get a little dry if they have no outlet for loving, serving, and ministering to others. They are ready to learn the key to ministry, which is "everyone can minister who can love." Throughout the lesson, emphasize to kids the valid need for faithful love and kindness in the church and various ministries they could become involved in to express faithful love and kindness.

COVENANT TIME

Faithful Love, Kindness, and Respect (up to 10 minutes)

Have members of each family sit together and work on this activity with other members of their family.

Give each family a "Commitment to Kindness, Faithfulness, and Respect" handout (p. 65) and a pen. Say: **Now I'd like you to decide as a family how you can apply what you've learned today. Create a promise to each other by filling in the blanks on this handout. For example, you might say, "We will show more kindness to each other by going out of our way to serve one another by giving massages, serving snacks to one another, and by trying to make one another feel special," "To more faithfully show love to one another, we will smile more at one another, say 'I love you!' more, not blame one another, and not cut one another down," and "We will show respect to each other by listening to each other's ideas and opinions and not ridicule or be sarcastic."**

Give families a few minutes to create their covenants, and then say: **When you're finished, sign your names and write the date at the bottom. Take this covenant home with you, and post it someplace where everyone will see it on a daily basis.**

Now I'd like you to close in prayer with your family. Take a moment to pray for God to help the person on your left to be kind, faithful, loving, and respectful and to stick to the promises made in the covenant. Have families pray as you have directed.

OPTIONAL SNACK TIME

Serve blueberry muffins with your smoothies.

Story of RUTH

The story of Ruth took place during a time in Israel's history when the judges governed. It was a time of idol worship and unfaithfulness to God.

In the beginning of the story of Ruth, a man named Elimelech, his wife Naomi, and their two sons left Israel to live in nearby Moab because of a crisis—there was no food for them to eat.

Discuss these questions:

• **What do you think it would be like to have no food to eat at all?**

• **How did this family seem to hold up in these tough circumstances? Why?**

Let's continue with the story to see what happened next.

Elimelech, Naomi, and their sons found food in Moab. But while they were living there, a series of terrible things happened.

Read Ruth 1:3-5 to find out what happened.

In the face of these terrible crises, Naomi decided to return to her homeland in Bethlehem. She tried to convince both of her daughters-in-law to go back to their parents so that each could find a new husband.

Read Ruth 1:14-18 to see what happened next.

Discuss these questions:

• **What does Naomi's decision to encourage her daughters to return to their own people tell you about Naomi?**

• **What does Ruth's determination to go with her mother-in-law tell you about Ruth and about her relationship with Naomi?**

• **How did Ruth show Naomi faithful love and kindness?**

• **Tell of a time when someone in our family showed faithful love and kindess to you. Explain.**

• **Tell of a time when you believe you showed faithful love to a family member or were especially kind. Explain.**

63

Let's continue with our story.

Naomi and Ruth journeyed to Bethlehem and were greeted by Naomi's relatives and friends.

One of Naomi's relatives in Bethlehem owned a field. Since it was time for the barley harvest, Ruth went to glean in the fields. Ruth came to the field owned by Boaz, where she met him for the first time. This begins one of the most beautiful and famous love stories of all time.

Read Ruth 2:4-17 to find out how Boaz treated Ruth.

Ruth was a Gentile. A Gentile is someone who isn't a Jew. In those days, Jews didn't usually treat Gentiles with kindness and respect, because Gentiles didn't believe in the God of Israel or live by the same rules and cultural ideas. Still, Boaz was kind and respectful to Ruth.

Discuss these questions:

- **Why do you think Boaz was kind and respectful to Ruth?**

- **How kind and respectful are you toward all members of our family, even the ones you don't know very well? Explain.**

When Ruth told Naomi of all of these kindnesses, Naomi encouraged Ruth to get to know Boaz better. Ruth went to meet Boaz and told him she wanted him to marry her!

Read Ruth 3:10-11 to learn how Boaz reacted when Ruth told him what she wanted.

Read Ruth 4:13-17 to see how the story ends.

God honored Ruth's faithfulness and kindness by not only giving her a husband and children in her new homeland, but by allowing her to be the great-grandmother of David and part of the direct lineage to Jesus!

Commitment to
KiNDNESS, FAiTHFULNESS, and RESPECT

• **We will show more kindness to each other by...**

• **To more faithfully show love to one another, we will...**

• **We will show respect to each other by...**

Name _____ **Date** _____

Name _____ **Date** _____

Name _____ **Date** _____

Name _____ **Date** _____

Sticking Together

Ruth and Naomi

LESSON 7

TEXT:
Ruth 1–4

LESSON FOCUS:

Family members should support one another through good times and bad times.

OBJECTIVES:

Family members will
- recognize the importance of family members sticking together during tough times,
- explore examples of supportive behavior in the story of Ruth and Naomi,
- identify the attitudes that will help the family stick together, and
- commit to strengthening their family by sticking together more closely.

STUFF YOU WILL NEED:

Bibles; refrigerator magnets (you may want to have each person bring one); chalk and a chalkboard; and, for each family, a sheet of heart or star stickers, a pen, a "We'll Stick Together" handout (p. 73), construction paper, scissors, markers, tape or glue, and a "Family Shield" handout (p. 74).

GATHERING ACTIVITY

Magnetic Force

As people arrive, distribute refrigerator magnets. When everyone has arrived, explain that each family should form a circle. Say: **Instead of holding hands, hold out your refrigerator magnets so they stick to the magnets of the family members beside you.**

Explain that you'll give families some instructions and that their goal is to follow the instructions while never allowing their magnets to separate. Say: **If any magnet becomes separated, continue with the activity but give yourself one point. We'll see who still has zero points by the end of the game.**

When everyone understands, call out the following instructions, allowing time between each instruction for families to respond:

- **Walk clockwise in a circle together.**
- **Take a bow together as a family.**
- **Do a chorus line kick together.**
- **Do the "wave."**

For an extra challenge, have families repeat the activities with their eyes closed. Afterward, ask families to raise their hands if they were able to stick together through all the activities. Lead everyone in a round of applause whether families raise their hands or not. Then lead a discussion with the whole group, asking:

- **What was easy about this activity? What was difficult?**
- **What are some things—good and bad—that can threaten to separate families?**
- **What does "sticking together as a family" mean to you?**
- **Why do you think it's important for families to stick together?**

Say: **Families are gifts from God that provide protection and support. Family members who are threatened by good or bad life events are made stronger when they stick together with other family members. Family members should support one another through good times and bad times. We'll look in the Bible today at an example of a family that stuck together.**

BIBLE STORY TIME

We'll Stick Together

(up to 20 minutes)

Distribute a sheet of heart or star stickers, a pen, and a "We'll Stick Together" handout (p. 73) to each family. Say: **There are few stories of loyalty in the world as powerful as the story of Ruth and Naomi. As you explore this story, look for examples of family members sticking together and supporting one another. Each time you find an example, give each other a sticker to wear, and underline the example on your handouts.**

When everyone has finished the handout, ask volunteers to share how many stickers they used and to share some of the examples they found of family members sticking together and supporting one another. Then have families go through the handout again and put check marks when they find an event that could or did separate family members. Ask:

• **How did the Bible characters in this story respond when something threatened to separate them?**

• **What difference did it make in Ruth's life that she stuck with Naomi?**

• **What difference did it make in Naomi's life that Ruth stuck with her?**

• **What difference did it make in both Naomi's and Ruth's lives that Naomi's family members welcomed her back?**

• **What can we learn from Naomi and Ruth for our own families?**

Say: **Without Ruth, Naomi may not have had the support she needed after her husband and sons died. But Ruth loved Naomi and stuck by her. Ruth and Naomi supported each other and stuck with one another as family members should.**

FAMILY LEARNING ACTIVITY

Family Shields

(up to 20 minutes)

Say: **We can learn from Ruth and Naomi several qualities that will help us protect our families from separation.** Explain that each family will read several Scriptures and then will create a family shield

Field-Test FINDINGS

Encourage parents to save the lesson handouts in a file folder or a notebook so they can refer to them later.

to protect them from separation.

Distribute Bibles, construction paper, scissors, markers, tape or glue, and a "Family Shield" handout (p. 74) to each family. Give families ten to fifteen minutes to create their shields. As families work, write the following questions on the chalkboard. When time is up, each family should discuss the questions. Ask:

• How is it that qualities on our shields (honor, love, unselfishness, willingness to help) protect our family?

• Tell of a time in our family when you felt especially honored, loved, treated unselfishly, or helped by someone in our family. Explain how you felt.

• Why is it so important for family members to honor one another? to love one another? to treat one another unselfishly? to help one another?

Give families five minutes for discussion, and then gather all families together as one big group. Have each family explain its shield to another family.

Say: As we live out the qualities on our shield toward one another, we will protect one another and we will show we are sticking close to one another. Through good times and bad times we really do need one another. We really must stick together.

Ask:

• What was the most positive and encouraging story someone in your family group shared in the last discussion (a time the person felt especially loved, honored, helped, or treated unselfishly by another family member)?

• How can our families become "stickier" and our shields become stronger?

• What will it cost each one of us to make our family stickier (what effort or sacrifice would be required)?

Say: I believe all our families could become stickier. I believe all of us want to be more loving, honoring, unselfish, and helpful toward one another. I believe we all want to be there for one another in the good times and the bad times.

COVENANT TIME

Strengthening the Shield

(up to 10 minutes)

Say: Let's see what can happen if we are not careful to stay sticky with one another during good times and bad times.

Have each family stand in a separate circle, facing each other and holding hands. Say: **When we say things that hurt each other, it pulls us apart. If you've said something that hurt someone in your family this week, let go of others' hands.** As they separate during this activity, family members should also drop hands.

When we make fun of someone in our family, it separates us. If you've made fun of someone in your family this week, take two steps back.

When we refuse to take part in the work of the family, we create additional work and pressure for others. If you haven't done your fair share of the family's work this week, turn around.

When we don't share with one another, we create jealousy. If you haven't shared, take two steps forward if you just turned around, backward if you didn't just turn around.

But when we choose to say things that help and protect each other, we grow closer. If you've shown love and honor to a family member this week, turn and face your family (if necessary).

If you've helped a family member this week, take four steps toward your family.

Whether or not you've shared anything with a family member this week, join with your family right now in a family hug.

Have each family separately commit to strengthening the Family Shield they created.

Say: On the back of your Family Shield handout, each family member should write or draw one thing he or she will do to strengthen the Family Shield through loving, honoring, helping, or somehow being unselfish and serving. For example, a child might commit to help a younger brother or sister develop a writing, drawing, or sport skill. Someone else might commit to helping with the dishes every day without being asked.

When families have finished writing their commitments on the back of their Family Shield, have them form separate family circles.

FOR Younger KIDS

Younger children would really enjoy seeing the story of Ruth and Naomi presented with puppets or live actors.

FOR Older KIDS

Since older kids may be *looking* for a little more family separation, you might suggest that families with older kids discuss positive and negative types of separation. For example, while it may be OK for kids to spend more time with friends, it may not be OK for them to sacrifice family dinners to spend time with friends.

Say: Now pray for God to help your family stick together even more closely through the good times and the bad times. As you pray, pass the shield around the circle. As each person holds the shield, he or she should pray for God's strength to keep the commitment.

OPTIONAL SNACK TIME

Have families make "shields" with graham crackers and frosting. Distribute graham crackers, bowls or tubes of frosting, plastic knives, and napkins. Explain that on the front of each "shield" (graham cracker), each family member can draw with the frosting the area of the family shield he or she will strengthen.

We'll STICK TOGETHER

(BASED ON Ruth 1–4)

The book of Ruth in the Bible tells the story of a woman's family. The woman's name was Naomi. Her husband died, but she still had two sons. They lived far away from Naomi's homeland. When each son got married, Naomi had two daughters-in-law.

Later, both of Naomi's sons died, and Naomi felt alone. She wanted to return to her homeland, so she told her daughters-in-law to return to their own families, too. One daughter-in-law did, but one refused. Her name was Ruth, and she loved Naomi. She said to Naomi, "Don't urge me to leave you or to turn back from you. Where you go I will go, and where you stay I will stay. Your people will be my people and your God my God." So Ruth stayed with Naomi, and they traveled together to Naomi's homeland.

When Ruth and Naomi got to Naomi's homeland, everyone was excited to see them. Naomi told them how sad she was that her husband and sons had died.

Naomi and Ruth had to take care of themselves, so Ruth went into the fields to gather grain to eat. While there, she met one of Naomi's relatives, a respected man named Boaz. He was kind to Ruth and encouraged her to gather grain from his fields and drink from his water jars. Boaz also told his men to be kind to Ruth and to leave grain for her. Because of Boaz's kindness, Ruth was able to provide plenty of food for Naomi and herself.

Naomi wanted Ruth to marry again, so she wisely advised Ruth to approach Boaz in a respectful manner. Boaz was pleased and promised to care for Ruth and Naomi.

Boaz and Ruth were married, and they cared for Naomi, who was like a grandmother to their children. The women of the town celebrated with Naomi that her sadness had turned to joy. They said, "Praise be to the Lord…for your daughter-in-law, who loves you and who is better to you than seven sons."

family shield

From the supplies you have, create a Family Shield that reflects these four elements.

Love

protects families from separation.

Read Ruth 1:16.

Read John 13:34.

Create one section of your shield to illustrate your family's love.

Working together

and a willingness to help protect families from separation.

Read Ruth 2:17-18; 3:1.

Read Ephesians 4:2-3.

Create one section of your shield to illustrate how your family works together.

Honoring one another

protects families from separation.

Read Ruth 2:11-13.

Read Philippians 2:3-4.

Create one section of your shield to illustrate how you show honor to one another.

Sharing

and unselfishness protect families from separation.

Read Ruth 3:15-17.

Read Acts 4:32.

Create one section of your shield to illustrate how your family shares.

74

Open Lines of Communication

Hannah and Her Family

SESSION FOCUS:

Communicating with God requires both speaking and listening.

OBJECTIVES:

Family members will

• practice communication skills by identifying items by sound;

• realize communication goes beyond spoken language to body language, facial expressions, and more;

• evaluate and draw practical tips from how Hannah, Samuel, Elkanah, Eli, and God communicated;

• develop two-minute "seminars" on communicating with God, then talk to and listen to God; and

• commit to communicate with God individually and as families.

STUFF YOU WILL NEED:

Bibles; paper; markers or crayons; chalk and a chalkboard; and, for each family, "Communication Central" handouts (p. 81) and a pen; and, for each group of six, a bag containing a blindfold and at least five of the following items: paper, an apple, a bouncy ball, a pair of dice, a deck of cards, a bell, a balloon, a snack-sized bag of potato chips, a piece of bubble gum, a plastic bag, a full can of soda, or other items that make sounds. (Note: Ideally each bag should contain five different items, and no two bags should be exactly alike.)

GATHERING ACTIVITY

Listening Test

(up to 15 minutes)

Have everyone sit together in groups of six. Distribute a bag of items to each group. Allow each group to choose one member to put on a blindfold. Then have another group member reach into the bag and pull out one item.

Say: **The object is for the blindfolded person to guess the item you have chosen from the bag. To do this, the group member with the chosen item should make a sound with the item he or she pulled from the bag. For example, if you're holding a piece of gum, you could unwrap the gum, chew it loudly, and blow a bubble. Spend only a few seconds making the sound, and then ask the blindfolded person to identify the object. The person has up to thirty seconds to guess the item.**

After the first blindfolded person has had up to thirty seconds to guess the item, allow other family members to put on the blindfold and test their listening skills. After everyone has had a turn, ask:

• **Which sounds were easy to identify? Which sounds were difficult? Why?**

• **What made this activity difficult? easy?**

• **What kinds of things distracted you from listening and hearing?**

• **What did this activity teach you about how to listen?**

• **How was listening to and trying to decipher the sounds like listening for God?**

Say: **Communication requires someone to listen. It also requires someone to speak. Let's test our speaking skills now by telling each other what kind of week it has been.**

Unspoken Motion Language

(up to 10 minutes)

Explain that each person must find at least three people outside his or her family and tell those people what kind of week it has been.

Say: **The catch is that each time you must use a different style of "speaking"—body language, facial expressions, and spoken language, for example. You cannot speak the same way twice.**

When everyone understands the directions, have people walk around the room and "speak" to others about their week. After everyone has finished, have families gather again. Ask:

• **What was the most comfortable way for you to speak? the most uncomfortable? Why?**

• **From these listening and speaking activities, what do you think good communication involves?**

• **Based on your definition of good communication, do you think you communicate well with God? Explain.**

Say: At the very least, communication requires that someone speak and someone listen. That's true for our communication with other people *and* with God. Today we'll discover a biblical example of a family that communicated with God.

BIBLE STORY TIME

Communication Central

(up to 20 minutes)

Have everyone separate into families. Each family should sit in a circle. Distribute a Bible, a pen, and "Communication Central" handouts (p. 81) to each family. Though all family members will receive a handout, family members should probably work together on the same sheet. Explain that the handout will help families learn how Hannah and others communicated. They will do this by noting all the ways people spoke and listened in three passages of Scripture: 1 Samuel 1:1-20; 2:1; and 3:1-21.

Give families ten to fifteen minutes to complete the handouts. As they work, write the following questions, as well as the unfinished statements and questions in the Family Learning Activity section, on the chalkboard. After families have completed the handout, have them discuss the questions below within their families. Ask:

• **With which character did you most identify?**

• **What did you find to be most uplifting in these Bible passages?**

• **How were Hannah's and Samuel's lives changed by their communication with God?**

• **What can your family learn from Hannah's and Samuel's examples of communication with God?**

Have volunteers jump up and quickly report to the whole group what they've learned about communication—especially communication with God.

Field-Test FINDINGS

Provide Bibles in an easy-to-read translation for parents and kids to use together.

FAMILY LEARNING ACTIVITY

Rapid Recall

(up to 15 minutes)

Families should still be sitting separately.

Say: **Now let's practice listening to each other for a few minutes. Family members should each take up to thirty seconds to complete the following unfinished statements while the family listens:**

• **I would describe my communication with God as…**

• **What I would most like to learn from these Bible accounts in my own communication with God is…**

• **To incorporate more listening into my communication with God I could…**

When families have finished talking, have each family member complete one of the unfinished statements above in the way he or she recalls one family member responded. Ask:

• **After hearing us recall what others said, what grade would you give us on our speaking? our listening?**

• **Why do you think it is important to have two-way communication with God, both speaking and listening?**

Communication Seminars

(up to 10 minutes)

Explain that each family will develop a two-minute "seminar" on improving communication with God that they'll share with one other family. Encourage families to create titles for their seminars to summarize what good communication with God requires; to create a motto or advertising slogan; and to create a two-minute seminar presentation that involves the whole family. The seminar should explain what the most important things to remember are as we communicate with God (based on what they learned in the lesson) and the benefits to them of healthy two-way communication with God.

Give families five minutes to develop their seminars, and then call time. Have each family perform its seminar for one other family.

After each family has performed its seminar, have everyone gather together and turn their attention to you. Ask:

• **What is the one thing that stands out most in your mind from**

FOR Younger KIDS

Encourage families with younger children to emphasize that communicating with God means talking and listening to God just as they talk and listen to people. Point out that Hannah did not have to know certain words to speak to God; she told God what she felt in her heart. Also point out that Samuel was very young when God spoke to him, so God doesn't speak only to adults.

Suggest that families with younger children discuss more concrete questions such as "What did Hannah say? Why?", "What did God do when Hannah prayed?", "What happened because Hannah talked to God?", "What happened because Samuel listened to God?", and "What do you want to tell God?"

what you have learned in today's lesson? Why?

• How can improved communication with God benefit you and your family?

• How can you improve the way you speak to God as an individual? as a family?

• How can you improve the way you listen to God as an individual? as a family?

Say: It is so incredible for us to be reminded that God desires to speak to our hearts and offer us guidance and assurances of his love. Prayer is not just us talking to God but God listening and responding to us. What a precious privilege it is to communicate with God.

COVENANT TIME

Practice Makes Perfect
(up to 10 minutes)

Have families sit separately again. Distribute paper and markers or crayons to each family. Say: **Now let's practice communicating with God. Each family member should write or draw a prayer to God on their paper. Think about Hannah's prayers as you write or draw. Maybe you need to talk to God about a problem you're facing, or maybe you'd like to praise and thank God for something wonderful in your life. Whatever your prayer is, take two minutes now to talk to God on paper.**

After about two minutes, say: **Now let's practice listening to God. Think about how Samuel listened to God, accepting God's message by saying, "Speak, for your servant is listening." Let's listen now.**

After two minutes of listening, ask families to create a covenant to communicate with God on a regular basis—both as individuals and as families.

Have each family draw on one sheet of paper outlines of family members' hands. Then have each person write in one handprint how he or she will communicate with God on a regular basis—praying and listening alone every morning before breakfast, for example. Then have each person write in another handprint how the entire family will communicate with God on a regular basis—holding hands and praying and listening every evening before bed, for example.

FOR Older KIDS

Older kids' schedules are filling up, and they may have a difficult time understanding that communication with God should be a priority. Encourage healthy habits in older kids by asking them to consider the advantages of stopping and talking and listening to God. Ask them to consider how Hannah's life changed and how Samuel's life changed when they communicated with God.

After families have finished their covenants, ask them to pray as families, asking for God to help them speak to him and listen to him well. Suggest that each family member tell God about the specific commitment he or she has made.

Remind families to take home their "praying hands" covenants as reminders of their communication commitments.

OPTIONAL SNACK TIME

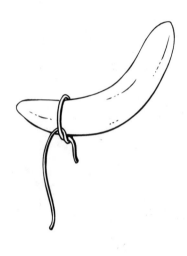

Have everyone make "telephones" to eat. Distribute bananas, paper plates, a plastic knife, and red licorice strings to each family. Have families cut the bananas lengthwise and give one banana half to each family member as a "telephone receiver." Then explain that they can tie a licorice string to each banana half as the "telephone cord."

COMMUNICATION CENTRAL

Read 1 Samuel 1:1-20; 2:1; 3:1-21.
As you read, draw lines of communication on the diagram below.

Draw a solid line to show that someone spoke. ─────────────

Draw a dashed line to show that someone listened and responded. ----------------------

In each box, write your family's thoughts about:
• how carefully and responsively each listened to other people,
• how clearly and respectfully each spoke to other people,
• how carefully and responsively each listened to God (if applicable), and
• how clearly and respectfully each spoke to God (if applicable).

```
┌─────────────────┐              ┌─────────────────┐
│  HANNAH         │              │  ELKANAH        │
│                 │              │                 │
│                 │              │                 │
│                 │    ┌─────────────────┐         │
│                 │    │                 │         │
└─────────────────┘    │                 │         │
                       │    GOD          │─────────┘
                       │                 │
┌─────────────────┐    │                 │    ┌─────────────────┐
│  SAMUEL         │    │                 │    │         ELI     │
│                 │    └─────────────────┘    │                 │
│                 │                           │                 │
│                 │                           │                 │
│                 │                           │                 │
└─────────────────┘                           └─────────────────┘
```

Wise Beyond His Years

Josiah

TEXT:
2 Kings 22:1–23:3

LESSON FOCUS:

God gives wisdom to people of all ages.

OBJECTIVES:

Family members will
- recognize the difference between wisdom and knowledge;
- teach one another, showing that God gives people of all ages wisdom;
- learn from Josiah's example that wisdom begins with recognizing right from wrong and doing what is right;
- recognize the wisdom they've received from God and the wisdom they need from God; and
- commit to pray for a partner's wisdom needs.

STUFF YOU WILL NEED:

Bibles; pennies; pens; and a "Josiah's Wisdom" handout (p. 89), scissors, and a "Wisdom Source Puzzle" handout (p. 90) for each family.

GATHERING ACTIVITY

The Guessing Game

(up to 15 minutes)

As everyone arrives, have them form groups of five or six people each. Give one member of each group a penny. Each group should then form a circle. Say: **We're going to begin today by testing how wise you are.** Instruct each person to whom you gave a penny to hold the penny in one hand and put both hands behind his or her back. Tell people to the penny-holders' right to guess which hand the penny is in. Ask for people who guessed correctly to raise their hands. When they do, say: **Wow! You sure are wise!** Groups should continue passing the penny around the circle, repeating the exercise until everyone has had a chance to guess which hand the penny is in.

Ask:

- **Was this truly a test of wisdom? Why or why not?**
- **How do people show true wisdom in real life?**
- **How would you define "wisdom"?**

Say: **Now you're really going to get a chance to show how wise you truly are!** Have everyone pair up with a partner, preferably not with someone close to their age. All should seek an older/younger pairing.

Wisdom Begins With Knowing Right and Wrong

(up to 10 minutes)

Say: **I am going to read a number of statements. If you believe the statements are right, stand and thrust your fist into the air and semi-shout, "Right!" If the statement is wrong, shake your head "no" vigorously and say in your deepest voice, "Wrong!" After each statement you will turn to your partner and simply ask "Do you ever do this?" and your partner should simply answer yes or no.** Read the statements from the "Right or Wrong?" box on page 85.

Right or Wrong?

1. It's OK to steal someone else's Eggo waffle.
2. If you're upset with someone in the family, don't talk to them about it, just be mean to them for a day or two.
3. It's OK to lie to your parents for a good reason.
4. It's a good thing to tell others in the family that you love them and to give them hugs and kisses.
5. It is a good thing to regularly encourage and "cheer on" other family members.
6. The idea at home is to try and get out of as many jobs and chores as possible.
7. Leaving cards and notes telling other family members why they are special to us is unnecessary.
8. Family time should be a priority on our time and commitments.
9. It is OK to gossip about family members to those outside the family—to tell others bad things about a family member.
10. Family members should respect one another and make one another feel special.

After everyone has responded to the statements, ask:

• How easy was it for you to determine right and wrong in this game?

• How much advantage did it give you to be your age? Why?

• Think of the question your partner asked you after each statement, "Do you ever do this?" How satisfied were you with the answers you were able to give to this question? Why?

• Why is it important to not just know what is right to do, but to actually do the right things?

Say: Wisdom is different from knowledge and intelligence. You can have the highest I.Q. in the world and still not be wise. And no matter what our age, we can all have wisdom. Wisdom is knowing the right thing to do and doing it. God gives wisdom to people of all ages—even very young people. In fact, today we're going to learn about a young boy to whom God gave great wisdom.

BIBLE STORY TIME

Wisdom at Any Age

(up to 20 minutes)

Have people get into their family groups. Distribute Bibles, a pen, and a "Josiah's Wisdom" handout (p. 89) to each family. Have family members work together to complete their handouts.

When families have completed their handouts, ask them to take turns presenting their speeches before the entire class. Encourage every member of the family to participate in presenting the speeches. Afterward, have everyone enthusiastically applaud the speeches. The group should remain together for a discussion. Ask:

• How did Josiah show wisdom?

• Why is wisdom important for everyone to have, not just a king like Josiah?

• What difference do you think it made to the people that Josiah led them wisely?

Say: Even though Josiah became king at such a young age, he "did what was right in the eyes of the Lord." He knew what was right, and he did it. And that's what true wisdom is—at any age.

FAMILY LEARNING ACTIVITY

Wisdom: Going the Right Way

(up to 20 minutes)

Have the group remain together for the first part of this activity. Ask people to respond to the following questions with a show of hands. Each time you ask about a task, ask those who respond to name the source of their wisdom—how they learned to do the task right.

Ask:

Who knows how to do the following things correctly:

• change the oil in a car?

• bake cookies?

• change a baby's diaper?

• use a computer?

• play video games?

• mow the lawn?

• make dinner?

• What role do you think God plays in helping us gain wisdom when we need it?

• What sources do you believe God can use to provide us with wisdom to do right?

Say: James 1:5 says, "If any of you lacks wisdom, he should ask God, who gives generously to all without finding fault, and it will be given to him." It is good to know that God is willing to provide us with wisdom and that he has many ways of doing so.

Wisdom Source Puzzle

(up to 10 minutes)

Say: In just a moment you will separate from the group into your family groups. Each of you will be given three or more puzzle pieces. On your puzzle pieces you should write or draw a source of wisdom for you (such as the Bible, a parent, or a teacher) and then draw a picture or write in one sentence a specific example of how God used that source in the past to give you wisdom (perhaps he provided wisdom when you considered a career change or helped you know how to handle a difficult relationship problem). It's OK if sources are duplicated. You will then assemble the puzzle as each of you shares what you wrote. As your pieces are needed, you are to share what you wrote on that piece.

Have families gather separately from the large group. Distribute pens, scissors, and a "Wisdom Source Puzzle" handout (p. 90) to each family. One family member should cut apart the puzzle pieces on the family's handout. You may want to repeat the instructions after you distribute the handouts.

When everyone has finished writing, have families gather as a large group. Ask:

• What are some of the many sources of wisdom God has used to get us wisdom in our lives?

• What does your family puzzle say about the wisdom of your family as a whole? about God's wisdom?

• Tell us of a time when God provided you with wisdom when you needed it most. What source of wisdom did he use to get you the wisdom (such as a parent or a friend)?

• Why do you think God wants to give us wisdom?

field-Test FINDINGS

Consider developing optional "homework." Some families may request more family activities during the week between lessons.

Say: **Today we learned that God gives wisdom to people of all ages—and that includes every person in our own families! Wisdom grows in us over time as we look to God and recognize all the sources he provides to give us wisdom. When we're wise, we do what God wants us to do, we do what we know is right to do.**

COVENANT TIME

Wisdom Partners
(up to 10 minutes)

While the large group is still together, provide the following instructions for the Covenant Time activity.

Say: **Have someone in your family read 1 Timothy 4:12, then ask:**

• **How does this verse apply to Josiah? to each of us?**

Say: **God gives wisdom to people of all ages, so we can all encourage each other and help each other grow wiser! In just a moment you will meet again with just your family. When you do, share with them one area or situation in your life where you most need God's wisdom right now—maybe you're going through a real problem or crisis or maybe you just need guidance for a tough decision. Whatever it is, share it. Then pick up a puzzle piece that names a source of wisdom you believe God may well use to help you in this situation. Then pray together as a family for each of your wisdom needs.**

Give families up to five minutes to do this. When families have finished praying, encourage each family member to form a prayer partnership with at least one other family member. These prayer partners should agree to pray for one another and their wisdom needs each day of the next week.

OPTIONAL SNACK TIME

Have everyone make a "king's crown" to eat—not to wear! Give each person half a bagel, and set out cream cheese, plastic knives, napkins, and colorful "jewels" such as grape halves, strawberry slices, and blueberries. Allow everyone to decorate a crown with jewels and then gobble up the crown.

Josiah's Wisdom
(Based on 2 Kings 22:1–23:3)

Instructions:

Read the following overview of Josiah's story. As you read, think about what Josiah did to show wisdom.

Josiah was only eight years old when he became king of Israel!

• **How would you feel if you became king when you were eight years old?**

• **What are some things you think would be most important to do if you became king?**

The Bible says Josiah "did what was right in the eyes of the Lord." God gave Josiah wisdom at a young age.

While Josiah was king, the high priest discovered an old book in the temple—the Book of the Law that God had given Josiah's ancestors. When Josiah heard what the book said, he was very troubled. He realized that he and his people had failed to do what God commanded in his Word. Josiah knew what he had to do! He knew he must lead his people to obey God's Word.

Josiah called together all the people of Jerusalem. He read to them God's Word and promised to the Lord in front of all the people that he would do what God had commanded. Then, following his example, all the people also promised to do what God had commanded. What do you think Josiah told the people on the day he publicly made his promise to God?

• **With your family, write a short speech that Josiah might have made that day.**

The speech should reflect that Josiah was so wise that all the people of Jerusalem followed his example. Refer to 2 Kings 23:1-3 for a general idea of what the speech was about. Be sure everyone in your family contributes a sentence or two to the speech. Use the space below to write the speech.

Wisdom Source
P U Z Z L E

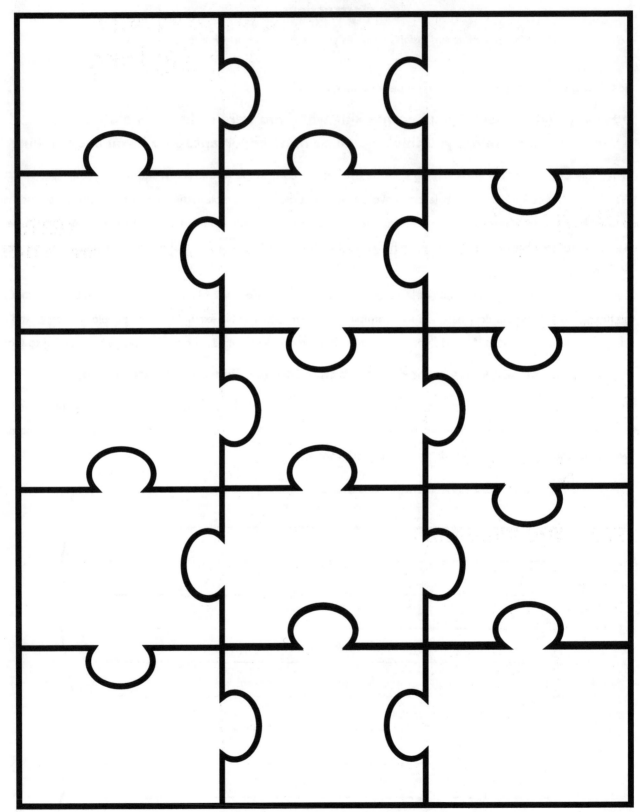

All in the Family

Jesus' Mother and Brothers and Sisters

TEXT:
Mark 3:31-35

LESSON FOCUS:

We belong to an extended family made up of people who do God's will.

OBJECTIVES:

Family members will

• explore their family tree and the benefits of being in a family,

• learn the expanded version of "family" as Jesus defined it,

• recognize the benefits of having an extended family of believers, and

• commit to serving their families—including the expanded version of family.

STUFF YOU WILL NEED:

Bathroom tissue to use as blindfolds; pens; chalk and a chalkboard; and a Bible, a "Family Tree and Me" handout (p. 98), an "Extending the Family" box (p. 94), and a "Five Qualities of a Servant" handout (p. 99) for each family.

GATHERING ACTIVITY

family Search

(up to 15 minutes)

field-Test FINDINGS

Put all the "stuff" you'll need for each lesson in a large box. You may want to recruit a different family for each lesson to collect the materials you'll need and organize them in the box.

As people arrive, have them stand all together. Distribute rolls of bathroom tissue. Everyone should blindfold each other by wrapping bathroom tissue three or four times around their head, covering their eyes, and tying the blindfold behind their head.

After everyone has been blindfolded, have them begin milling about and greeting one another. Everyone should move slowly and carefully with arms crossed in front of their chest and with hands up at shoulder level. Finally, challenge everyone to try and be first to locate and stick with their family members. When family members find each other, they should form a train by placing their hands on the shoulders of another family member and following him or her. The only way family members can find one another is by asking, "Are you in my family?" to which the other person can only respond "uh-huh" (yes) or "uh-uh" (no). When families believe they have found all of their members, family members should shout together, "Family found!" After several rounds of this, have everyone remove their blindfolds and gather for a short discussion. Ask:

• **In this game, how did you determine who was in your family and who wasn't?**

• **Let's have some fun. If someone was trying to find your family by smell, what smell would they sniff for? by sound, what would they listen for? by sight, what would they look for?**

• **In real life, beyond saying "uh-huh" and sniffing around, how is it typically easier to determine who is in your family and who isn't?**

Say: Your family isn't just any family. It's special isn't it? Turn to someone who is not in your family, and tell them one of the best things about being in your family.

• **What are some things you heard others say they liked best about their family that really stood out to you? Why?**

Say: Our families are special aren't they? We just shared so many good things that we like best about them. What would we do without them? And you know what is really cool about families? It's that families have history. They go way back, all the way to Adam and Eve. Let's look at our family histories for a few minutes.

Family Tree and Me

(up to 10 minutes)

Have families gather separately. Distribute pens and the "Family Tree and Me" handouts (p. 98). Have families follow the instructions on the handout, consulting with one another on proper names of relatives and the words that best describe them. Family members may fill out their own copies if they choose. As families work individually to complete the family tree, write the following questions on the chalkboard for them to discuss when they are finished:

• **As you consider the words we used to describe our family members, how do you feel being a part of this family?**

• **What are some of the best things about being part of a family? (If we didn't have families, what would we miss out on?)**

• **What are some of the responsibilities of being part of a family?**

After five minutes or so, have some families share their responses to the questions you wrote on the board.

Say: **There are many great things about belonging to a family. Family members love each other and take care of each other and support each other. These are some of the benefits and the responsibilities we have toward our family members. And not just toward the family members we know of, but some additional members of our family tree as well—some members you probably didn't even think about when making your tree. You might be part of an even larger family tree than you thought!**

Have families keep their completed "Family Tree and Me" handout for use in the next activity.

BIBLE STORY TIME

Extending the Family

(up to 15 minutes)

Say: **Jesus expanded the definition of family to include a lot of other people. Let's see how this new definition came about.**

Have group members remain separated in their families. In their family groups, ask members to take turns telling of a time when their family members must have thought they were behaving strangely. For example, Dad could tell about the summer he was obsessed with a baseball hero and wouldn't stop talking about baseball. After everyone has shared, ask family members to take turns telling each other about a time their family members thought they were acting a little too important. For example, Mom might tell about a time she played the lead in the school play and insisted on being called "the star."

After everyone has shared, say to all: **Well, now you can understand what was going on in Jesus' family. He had been raised to be a carpenter, but he'd been away from home for a little while. When he came back, he was preaching—a respected profession that his family hadn't trained him for. The Bible says Jesus' family went to "take charge of him" because they thought he'd lost his mind! Jesus' response to his family provided us with a whole new definition of "family." Let's find out what happened.**

Families should remain separate. Distribute a Bible and a photocopy of the "Extending the Family" box below to each family, and give them five minutes to read the Scriptures, discuss the questions, and complete the activity.

When families have finished, have the group gather. Ask:
• **What was Jesus seeking to accomplish by saying whoever does**

Extending the Family

Read Galatians 3:26-28, and discuss these questions:
• **According to this passage, who are we through faith in Christ?**
• **What are the benefits (and responsibilities) of this?**

Read Mark 3:31-35, and discuss these questions:
• **Why do you think Jesus asked, "Who are my mother and my brothers"?**
• **How does Jesus expand the definition of family here?**
• **What do you think Jesus meant by "Whoever does God's will is my brother and sister and mother"?**

Add to the bottom of your completed "Family Tree and Me" handout several boxes side by side. Work together as a family to come up with three or four people whom family members feel close to and who meet the definition "Whoever does God's will" (and who are not already in your family tree). In each box, write the people's names and three words that best describe them just above the words "Our extended family" on the handout.

God's will is family—what was he trying to help us understand?

• In what way can this expanded definition of family affect how you'll treat others? Why?

Say: Jesus introduced a whole new way to look at family. Those who do God's will belong to his family—no exceptions. When we believe in Jesus, we become members of God's family. God is the head of the family, and other believers are our brothers and sisters. With such a big, loving family, we have lots of support and strength behind us!

Have families set aside their completed "Family Tree and Me" handouts to use in a later activity.

FAMILY LEARNING ACTIVITY

"New and Improved Family!" Commercials

(up to 20 minutes)

Have families separate from the group again.

Say: As a family you will develop a thirty-second "TV commercial" that presents the advantages of having an extended family of all those who do God's will ("new and improved!"). Your goal is to show the viewer why you think Jesus wants us to consider each other as a family.

Give families five to ten minutes to develop their commercials, and then have each family present its commercial to the large group. If your group is large or you don't have time for every family to present, have each family present its commercial to one other family.

After each family has presented its commercial, ask the group:

• What new benefits can we all enjoy as members of this extended family?

• What new responsibilities do we all face as members of this extended family?

Say: One of biggest responsibilities we have to our extended family is to serve its members. Let's explore some servant qualities so we can better care for and be more of a benefit to those in our extended family.

FOR Younger KIDS

Involving younger children in helping describe others can be a demanding task because of their limited verbal capability and difficulty understanding what it means to "describe." Break the question down and make it concrete by asking things like "How does (person's name) make you feel?", "What is something (person's name) does all the time?", and "What are some things (person's name) has told you?"

If youngsters become distracted or bored during a long discussion, have them draw pictures of the family members they know in the boxes on their copy of the "Family Tree and Me" handout.

Five Qualities of a Servant (up to 5 minutes)

Distribute the "Five Qualities of a Servant" handout (p. 99) to each family to discuss separately.

After everyone has completed the handout, bring them together, and ask:

• How did these qualities of a servant most challenge you?

• In what ways could you better serve those in your immediate and extended family?

Say: Jesus put God first by always doing God's will. He loved and he served without limits. As members of God's family, we're responsible for doing God's will, loving, and serving too. We serve God out of love and appreciation for who he is and what he's done for us. We also have lots of family members to love and look out for.

COVENANT TIME

I'll Do for You (up to 10 minutes)

Families should meet separately from the larger group. Have families look again at the "Family Tree and Me" handout. Ask families to make covenants to serve each part of their immediate and extended families, and then to write on the back of their family trees how they'll serve others. Encourage families to think of one way to serve each of the people they added to the bottom of their page as their extended family. For example, they might decide to write letters of appreciation for their example of Christ's love, to care for one of them who is sick, or to give the person a special gift.

When families have completed their covenants, ask them to pray together. Encourage each family member to pray for at least one other person or group listed on the family tree. Afterward, close by asking God to help each person accept his or her responsibilities as a member of God's family.

OPTIONAL SNACK TIME

Have extended family members practice serving each other during snack time. Serve a simple treat such as popcorn. Have the kids take the adults a paper towel full of popcorn, and have the adults take the kids a paper towel full of popcorn. Then have kids get the adults cups of water, and vice versa.

FOR Older KIDS

Encourage parents of older children to let their children take a key role in deciding how to serve others during the Covenant Time. Older kids will not only have wonderful ideas, but will also feel proud and special if their parents give them the responsibility to plan a service project.

Family Tree and Me

Instructions: Work together with your family to complete your family tree below. Fill in the names of each person and three words that best describe them. Parents should tell children a little bit about older relatives they may not have known.

Grandparents of mom (or stepmom)
(Great-Grandparents of children)

Grandparents of dad (or stepdad)
(Great-Grandparents of children)

Parents of mom (or stepmom)
(Grandparents of children)

Parents of dad (or stepdad)
(Grandparents of children)

Mom (or stepmom)
(Parent of children)

Dad (or stepdad)
(Parent of children)

Children

Our extended family

Five Qualities of a Servant

Instructions:

Read each of the qualities of a servant below. If you have time, look up the Scriptures that follow each one. (Otherwise that would be a good nightly mini-devotional activity for the next five days.) After you read each quality of a servant, discuss the following two questions:

- How would doing this for others be a blessing and benefit to them?

- What are some ways we could live out this servant quality for those in our extended family (those who do God's will who have faith in Christ)?

What is a servant? Someone who SERVES! A servant...

S erves others instead of himself or herself (Mark 9:35).

e qually treats others (Galatians 3:26-28).

r estores others (Galatians 6:1-2).

v alues others by treating them with respect (1 Timothy 5:1-2).

e nriches others (Ephesians 4:15-16).

It Takes All Kinds

John the Baptist, Elizabeth, and Zechariah

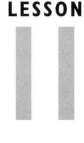

TEXT:
Luke 1:5-15a, 18-23,
57-66, 76-80

LESSON FOCUS:

God uses all kinds of people.

OBJECTIVES:

Family members will

- explore the unique way God used John the Baptist to point people to Jesus;
- discover that, like John, they can bear a spiritual "family resemblance" to Jesus;
- value and affirm the unique ways each family member has been used by God; and
- commit to allowing God to use them as a family this week.

STUFF YOU WILL NEED:

Old clothes, robes, fabric, scarves, belts, and sandals (or newspapers and masking tape); cardboard boxes; instrumental music CD or cassette; CD or cassette player; small boxes of chocolates (optional); index cards and pens; green or brown construction paper; scissors; chalk and chalkboard; and a roll of masking tape, a Bible, matches and a candle, glitter, modeling dough, fiberfill batting, a bowl of peanut butter, fifteen toothpicks, and a copy of the "John's Story" handout (p. 108) for each family.

GATHERING ACTIVITY

Desert Fashion Show

(up to 15 minutes)

Before class, gather "fashion" accessories families can use to assemble John the Baptist attire. Include a variety of old clothes, child-sized and adult-sized bathrobes, lengths of fabric, scarves, belts, and sandals. (You may want to ask families to supply some of these costume materials.) Assemble one box of costume accessories for every six people. As an easy option, just supply newspapers and masking tape, and people can use these instead of clothing and costume items. Then they can have a Newspaper Desert Fashion Show.

Welcome families as they arrive. Let them know everyone will be together for this opening activity. Point out the boxes of "fashion accessories" (costume materials or the newspaper and tape supplies). Say: **Today we are going to compete in a "Desert Fashion Show." Please get in groups of about six. When you've formed a group, select a box of "fashion accessories." Stand near your box.**

Help families form groups as necessary. When all the groups have selected a box, ask a volunteer to read Matthew 3:1-4 aloud. Say: **John the Baptist must have made quite a fashion statement as he walked around the desert covered in camel's hair. Let's see if we can recreate that desert look with a group display of desert fashions.**

Choose one person in your group to be a model, and then dress your model in true desert style using the fashion accessories provided. Your model can be a boy or a girl. After you've finished dressing your model, work together to come up with a script that describes your model's desert attire. For example, you might say, "Only the coolest desert dudes are wearing Bob's high-fashion leather sandals. They're specially crafted to let the sand flow through."

Allow time for groups to have fun dressing their models. Circulate among the groups to offer "fashion advice" as needed. When groups have finished assembling their outfits and composing their scripts, call everyone back together.

Turn on the CD or tape of instrumental "fashion show" music, and begin the Desert Fashion Show. Have the models parade down the "runway" one at a time. As each model displays his or her "ensemble," have another group member read the group's fashion script. Encourage applause after each model.

For added fashion fun, choose judges and award prizes for the "Best Desert Ensemble," "Most Like John the Baptist," or "Most Likely *Not* to be Seen on the Cover of Vogue magazine." Award chocolate-covered "ants" or "grasshoppers" (small boxes of chocolates) for the winning group. After the "fashion" show, lead a short discussion. Ask:

• **How would you describe some of the ensembles you saw modeled here today?**

• **What is perhaps the oddest way you have ever seen anyone dressed or behave (no names)? Describe what you saw. (Oh, and everyone here is exempt from being described.)**

• **How have you seen God use people in some exciting ways who were just a little different (in the Bible or in your experience)?**

• **How can someone be dressed outrageously, behave strangely, and still be very spiritual? Explain.**

Say: **John the Baptist may not have been a likely fashion model, but he definitely made God's "most likely to succeed" list. In spite of John's odd appearance, God used him to tell many people about Jesus. God uses all kinds of people. Let's find out more about how God used John.**

BIBLE STORY TIME

John's Story
(up to 20 minutes)

Before class, assemble the following items for each family: a candle and matches, glitter, modeling dough, a handful of fiberfill batting, a bowl of peanut butter, fifteen toothpicks, and a copy of the "John's Story" handout (p. 108). (If some family members have nut allergies, substitute another sticky or chewy food such as caramel candies.)

Families will work separately in the first part of this activity. Give each family a set of story items. Provide Bibles for families who need them. Say: **John the Baptist was quite a character. Your handout and the other items you've received will help you experience a little bit of John's story for yourselves.**

Family members should work together to complete the handout. After about five minutes, call families back together, and collect the supplies.

Ask:

• **What were some unusual circumstances surrounding the birth of John the Baptist?**

Have someone read Luke 1:76-80 aloud to the group again. Note that the first part of this passage is part of Zechariah's song for his son, John the Baptist.

• **What were some unusual characteristics of John's mission and ministry from this passage and from what else you know of him?**

• **What can we learn from how God used this very unusual man in some very significant ways?**

Say: Zechariah and Elizabeth and John weren't your typical family. Zechariah and Elizabeth were older than most other parents. And John turned out to be different than most other kids—how many people do you know who wear camel-hair shirts and eat locusts and honey? But God uses all kinds of people, even those who seem different.

FAMILY LEARNING ACTIVITY

Family Resemblance
(up to 15 minutes)

Have families pair up for the game part of this activity. Families should try and pair up with a family they know.

Say: **Let's explore the similarities and differences in the members of our families now. No two people are alike. Let's play a game now that will help us discover how different the members of our families are.**

Give each group index cards and pens. Have someone in the family give an index card and pen to each family member.

Say: **Think of two unique things about you that others even in your family might not know. Write or draw them on your card along with one more unique thing that isn't really true about you. For instance, you might write:**

• **It really upsets me when people come into my room without knocking.**

• **My favorite fast food is Taco Bell.**

• **I like Van Gogh's art.**

When everyone's finished, have one person collect the cards,

shuffle them, and read each one in turn. After reading the card, everyone in the family should vote on whose card they think it is. After that is known, the group should vote on which response of the three was false. If you want to make this a competition, give family members a point for every wrong vote. The highest score wins. If you don't understand, come see me. Everyone else can begin.

After the activity above is finished, have families separate and discuss the following questions. Either write the following questions on a chalkboard or copy them for individual families to discuss.

• Was it easy or hard to think of unique things about yourself? Explain.

• How is everyone in our family alike (physically, emotionally, spiritually, interests, talents)?

• How are you different from everyone else in our family?

• How well does our family do in respecting your unique qualities?

Allow a few minutes for families to complete their discussions, then call everyone back together.

Say: It's fun to notice the ways we're like our family members. When others notice similar physical features about our family, they often say we share a "family resemblance." Because John was Jesus' cousin, he may have physically resembled Jesus in some of these ways. But more important, John exhibited a spiritual "family resemblance" to Jesus. Like Jesus, John told people to stop doing bad things and follow God.

Ask:

• What makes a person show a "family resemblance" to Jesus?

• What "family resemblances" to Jesus might others notice about your family?

Say: During our time together, we've discovered that no two families in this room are exactly alike. We look different, act differently, and like to do different things. But even though our families are different, we all share a common goal of following Jesus.

God uses all kinds of people. It doesn't matter to God what kind of clothes we wear; where we live, work, or go to school; or what we do for recreation. What matters to God is what we do for Jesus. If we do the things Jesus wants us to do, God can use us! Let's celebrate the ways God can use us now.

COVENANT TIME

Locusts and Honey

(up to 10 minutes)

Younger children are just beginning to grasp the concept of family identity. They enjoy being identified as part of the family group, and they're fascinated by differences between families. Encourage families to use the activities in this lesson to help their young children see that serving God is a unique characteristic of their developing family identity.

Before class, cut green or brown construction paper into three-inch squares.

Set out the construction paper squares. Each family member will need a square for each person in his or her family. Give each family group a roll of masking tape.

Say: **The Bible tells us that John ate locusts and wild honey. John was a little different, but God used him to point the way to Jesus. To remind us that God can use us just as he used John, we're going to make our own "locusts" and "honey" right now.**

Hold up one of the construction paper squares. Say: **On your "locusts," write a word or draw a picture that tells one unique way God has used each person in your family. For example, if someone in your family befriended a new kid at school, you could write the new kid's name. If someone in your family helped serve food at a church dinner, you could draw a food item.**

Allow time for family members to complete their "locusts." Then have each family member wrap a piece of tape "honey" around an arm or leg, sticky side out. Tell family members to stick the "locusts" to the "honey" as they name the ways they've seen God use the members of their family.

Then have family groups work together to come up with a way they'll allow God to use their family this week. Have them write a word or draw a picture on a "locust" square to represent the action they'll agree to take. Then have each family member wrap another band of "honey" around his or her waist. Have family members attach their family "locusts" to their "honey" waistbands.

Have family groups join hands in a circle. Say: **Look at all these locusts hopping around! God really does use all kinds of people in all kinds of ways. Take a few moments now to pray about the ways God will use your family this week. Go around your circle, and have each person pray for the family member on his or her right. Thank God for the ways God has used that family member, then ask God to help your family point the way to Jesus, as John did.**

OPTIONAL SNACK TIME

Serve John the Baptist-style treats such as gummy worms, breakfast cereal with "honey" in the name, or chocolate and nut "turtles."

Older children can be extremely sensitive to seeming "different" from others. For this reason, they may not want to dress up as models in the Desert Fashion Show. Encourage older children to serve as "fashion designers" for younger children or adult models.

John's Story

1 **Read Luke 1:5-10.**
John's father, Zechariah, was a priest. In a lifetime, each priest was given only one opportunity to light the incense in the temple. Have a family member light your candle, and then have everyone take turns sharing their lifetime "highlights" of serving God.

2 **Read Luke 1:11.**
Shake some glitter around your candle to represent the angel that appeared to Zechariah near the altar. What would you do if you saw an angel and the angel spoke to you?

3 **Read Luke 1:12.**
Zechariah was "gripped with fear" when he saw the angel. Give each family member a piece of modeling dough. Use the dough to sculpt a reminder of something that really scared you. Tell your family how you felt during that scary time.

4 **Read Luke 1:14-15a.**
The angel told Zechariah that his son would be "a joy and delight." Reshape your modeling dough into something that makes you happy. Explain your dough sculpture to your family.

5 **Read Luke 1:18-19.**
Zechariah thought he and Elizabeth were too old to have a baby. Put some "gray hair" on each family member's head (or chin, for a beard), and then take turns telling why it might be hard for someone "well along in years" to take care of a baby.

6 **Read Luke 1:20-23.**
Because Zechariah didn't believe, the angel took away his speech. He couldn't talk. At a time when he wanted to tell everyone about the angel's promise and his soon-to-be-born son, he couldn't talk.

Put a fingerful of peanut butter in your mouth, and then tell your family members about the most exciting thing that happened to you this week. After you've swallowed your peanut butter, answer these questions: What was it like to try to talk when your mouth was full of sticky stuff? Do you ever get so excited you can hardly talk? How frustrated do you think Zechariah was with not being able to talk?

7 **Read Luke 1:57-66, 76-80.**
John's parents didn't give in to family pressure to call him by another name (probably Zechariah Jr.), but they obeyed God's command through the angel and named him "John." Use your toothpicks to spell out "John."

God spoke to Zechariah through an angel. How does God speak to us today? Tell about a time you obeyed one of God's commands.

Every time we obey God's commands, God can use us. Just as John grew "strong in spirit," we can grow strong in our faith by obeying God's commands. Silently pray, and ask God to help you obey his commands, and then blow out your candle.

The Runaway
The Prodigal Son and His Family

TEXT:
Luke 15:11-32

LESSON FOCUS:

All families need to forgive each other.

OBJECTIVES:

Family members will

• understand how holding on to unforgiveness causes harm,
• hear how one family in the Bible experienced forgiveness,
• explore ways that forgiveness and unforgiveness affect their family relationships, and
• covenant to forgive the members of their family.

STUFF YOU WILL NEED:

Bibles; chalk and chalkboard; black construction paper; scissors; and juggling objects (such as balls, beanbags, small plastic toys, or small stuffed animals), a Bible, a sheet of newsprint, a marker, tape or a glue stick, scissors, and black pens for each group.

GATHERING ACTIVITY

Group Juggle

Before class, gather enough juggling objects for each person to have one.

As family members arrive, direct them to stand all together in the center of the room. Say: **Today we are going to start with a Group Juggle!**

Have everyone form groups of four or six. Each group should stand in a circle. Have each group member number off and then switch places within their group circle. Help group members arrange themselves so they're standing across from, rather than next to, group members with adjacent numbers. (Ones across from twos, threes across from fours, and so forth.)

Give each person an object to juggle. Say: **Number Ones, throw your object to the Number Twos. Number Twos, as you're catching the Number One objects, throw your objects to the Number Threes. Number Threes catch from Number Twos and throw to Number Fours, and so on. You should always be catching and throwing. Let's practice once before we begin.**

After each group has had a chance to try the Group Juggle, let groups enjoy the game for a few minutes. Then call all groups back together, and collect the juggling objects. Hand each group a sheet of newsprint and a marker.

Invite groups to sit separately. Say: **On this paper, list the things this game might teach you about teamwork. Then list the things it could teach you about forgiveness. When your group has listed as many things as you can think of, raise your hands so I'll know you're finished.**

Allow a few minutes for groups to complete their lists. If groups seem stumped, ask them questions such as, "Did anyone drop their juggling object as you played?" or "How did family members respond?" When all the groups are ready, invite volunteers to share their responses and attach their newsprint to the wall for all to see. Ask:

• **When you were doing the Group Juggle, what did you need to do to succeed?**

• **How is that like or unlike what we need to do when we forgive someone?**

Say: When you were doing the Group Juggle, you had to constantly keep throwing and catching. If one person in your group had decided to hold on to his or her object instead of throwing it, the game wouldn't have worked. Forgiveness is like that. When you refuse to forgive someone, it's like holding on to something and refusing to let it go. And just as holding on to the juggling objects would have messed up our game, holding on to a grudge against someone and refusing to forgive can really mess up our relationships, especially our family relationships. All families need to forgive each other. Today we'll learn more about forgiveness.

BIBLE STORY TIME

Forgiveness Freezes

(up to 20 minutes)

Families will begin this activity working separately but will then join the larger group.

Before class, copy the list of Story Acts (p. 112) and corresponding Scripture references onto a chalkboard.

Say: **Today as we learn about forgiveness, we'll hear about a family in the Bible that needed to forgive. As you read the story, think about each character's words and actions. What did each person do wrong? What did each person do right? After everyone has had time to read the story, we'll go through it together and find out if any of the characters held on to bad feelings and refused to forgive.**

Have family groups read the Bible story from Luke 15:11-32 within their family groups. Invite groups to tell you what happened at the end of the story. Say: **At the end of this story, the father forgives his younger son and encourages his older son to do the same. Each family member in the story played an important part in this forgiveness drama. Let's freeze the camera and take a closer look at each person's actions now.**

Point out the list of Story Acts. Have each family group choose one act of the story and then work together to form a dramatic "frozen" scene of their story section's action. (Younger children may have an easier time understanding this if you compare it to putting a VCR on "pause.") Make sure at least one family works on each story act. If you have fewer than six family groups, assign some groups two of the shorter passages.

Story Acts

- Act 1: Persistent Son, Permissive Father (Luke 15:11-13)
- Act 2: No Food, No Money, No Friends (Luke 15:14-16)
- Act 3: Pig Sty Humility (Luke 15:17-20a—up to the point where the son leaves to go home)
- Act 4: Celebration! (Luke 15:20b-24—from the point where the father sees the son)
- Act 5: Unforgiveness and Jealousy (Luke 15:24-32)

Allow a few minutes for families to prepare their freezes. Then read the Bible story, one act at a time. After each act, stop and ask families to demonstrate their freezes. Ask the "unfrozen" families the following questions:

• What did the family members represented in this act do wrong? What did they do right?

• How did God use their right or wrong actions?

• What would have happened if the story stopped here?

After you've finished discussing the last act, say: If the story had stopped after any of the earlier acts, the relationships in this family could have been destroyed forever. The younger son might never have come home. The father might have wondered his whole life what had happened to his son. And the older son might have continued to hold a bitter grudge against his brother. But forgiveness changed this family's life.

Without forgiveness, the story would have ended in sadness. But because the father forgave his younger son and encouraged his older son to do the same, the story ends in joy and celebration. Listen to what else the Bible says about forgiveness.

Have a volunteer read Ephesians 4:32. Ask:

• How does reminding ourselves of all the times we've needed forgiveness make it easier to forgive others?

• How can remembering that God always forgives when we ask help us to forgive others?

Say: Through God we have an unlimited ability to forgive others. God can help us to be quick to forgive others no matter what the situation or offense. All families need to forgive each other. Let's spend some time doing that with our families now.

FAMILY LEARNING ACTIVITY

Forgiveness Links

(up to 20 minutes)

Though families will work separately on this activity, you will address the entire group at the beginning of it.

Before class, cut black construction paper into 2x6-inch strips. You'll need three or four strips for each family member.

Give each family group some black construction paper strips, tape or a glue stick, scissors, and black pens. Say: **All families need to forgive each other. When we don't forgive each other, our family relationships don't work right. All of the love and kindness we want to show to our family members is chained up inside, and it can't get out until we let go of our anger or hurt feelings and forgive.**

To symbolize how we can get chained up by unforgiveness, we'll make paper chains. On each link of the chain, write or draw a picture of something you need to forgive someone in your family for. Maybe you're still mad because someone else in your family took the last cookie. Or maybe a family member lost or threw away an important paper of yours. Make a chain link for each thing you think of.

Because the paper is black, no one else will know what you write unless you tell them. When you are done, connect your family's individual chains into a circle, and then raise your hands to let me know you've finished.

Allow time for families to work on their chains. If families or family members contend that they have no unforgiveness toward someone in the family, they can create their chain based on past unforgiveness, or you can broaden your comments to include unforgiveness toward others beyond the immediate family. When families finish, have them set the chains aside and discuss the following questions within their families. You may want to post the questions on a chalkboard.

• **Tell about a time when it was hard for you to forgive someone in our family. How did you feel before you forgave the person? How did you feel afterward?**

• How do you know when you've hurt someone in our family? How do you know when you need to forgive someone?

• What words or actions do we use when we need forgiveness from a family member? What words or actions do we use when we need to forgive?

After family groups have finished their discussions, call everyone back together. Invite families to share the positive words and actions they use when they forgive each other. Then say: **All families have times when they hurt each other. We're all human, and sometimes we do things—by accident or on purpose—that hurt the people we love. That's why all families need to forgive each other. Let's do an activity now that will help us see how forgiveness and unforgiveness can affect our families.**

Forgiveness Illustrated

(up to 5 minutes)

Have each family group form a circle, with family members facing each other. Lead the groups in the following exercise:

• **When we do things that hurt each other, we grow apart. Take two steps back from your circle.**

• **When we refuse to forgive or let go, we build a wall. Turn around and face out of your circle.**

• **When we keep remembering what someone did to us, we get stuck in a rut. Walk around your circle to the right.**

• **When we choose to forgive, we stop the cycle of unforgiveness. Stop walking around the circle.**

• **When we choose to forgive, we are free to love. Turn into your circle and hold hands.**

Say: **When we forgive quickly and make up, God is pleased. When we allow feelings of unforgiveness to remain in us unchallenged it tears us apart within ourselves and separates us from one another. Keeping hands held, pray silently to thank God for giving your family the gift of forgiveness.**

COVENANT TIME

Forgiveness Break

(up to 10 minutes)

Have families form separate circles for this activity. Say: **You now have the opportunity to agree together that for one week you will let go of whatever anger or hurt feelings you are holding against other family members. In your family, agree on a plan you'll use to work through any arguments or disagreements that come up this week. Agree to forgive.**

Allow a few minutes for families to discuss their forgiveness plans. Then have them retrieve the chains they made earlier. Say: **Before we start our forgiveness plans for the coming week, we need to "clear the slate" of any old hurts that might keep us from forgiving each other. Some of these old hurts are written on our "unforgiveness chains."**

In Isaiah 43:25, God tells us "I, even I, am he who blots out your transgressions, for my own sake, and remembers your sins no more." Look at the links on your chain. Can you see what you wrote? Probably not very well, if at all. The dark paper and ink have "blotted out" the hurts you wrote on your links. God's forgiveness is like that. God will forgive us so completely, he can't even remember the wrong things we've done. But first we have to ask.

Just as the younger son asked his father for forgiveness, we have to ask our family members to forgive us for the times we've hurt them. Take a few moments now to ask forgiveness from your family or individual family members. Choose at least one thing you wrote on your chain links, and ask the person you hurt to forgive you. Remember, your family members love you very much, so it's OK to be honest and open with them. All families need to forgive each other!

After everyone in your family has asked for and received forgiveness, take the paper chain you made, and place it around your family. Then break it together. Take the broken chain home to remind you that you've broken free from the hurt feelings that kept you from forgiving each other.

FOR YOUNGER KIDS

To make the concept of forgiveness easier for young children to understand, have families try this activity. Let younger children take turns wrapping themselves in the family chain. Have them try to hug another family member while they're wrapped up. Point out that just as the chains kept them from hugging each other, holding on to hurt feelings can keep us from loving each other. Then have the family remove the chains and give each other a group hug!

Older children often insist,
"That's not fair!" In situations
where forgiveness is called for,
they may be reluctant to offer
it until they're sure that the
offender also will be justly
punished. When older children
find themselves in these situations, encourage them to remember the story of the
prodigal son. Ask them who
they'd rather be like—the
younger brother who realized
his need for forgiveness, or the
older brother who refused to
forgive.

OPTIONAL SNACK TIME

Have families make a "rope" out of red licorice vines and then break them apart and eat them. Explain that the rope symbolizes sin and unforgiveness. Breaking the rope symbolizes forgiveness and letting go of any anger or hurt feelings family members may have toward each other.

Grandma's Treasure
Lois, Eunice, and Timothy

TEXT:
2 Timothy 1:5

LESSON FOCUS:

A positive Christian example goes a long way in building the faith of others.

OBJECTIVES:

Family members will
- realize that searching for those we can look up to and follow in the faith is similar to a treasure hunt,
- recognize how a sincere faith can be passed along in a family and how everyone in the family can be an influence on others,
- honor their "heroes" whom they most want to be like and whom they most look up to by discussing them and the qualities that make them such an inspiration and influence, and
- make a family commitment to be a more influential and inspirational example of Christ for others.

STUFF YOU WILL NEED:

Scissors, poster board (8½ x 11 inches), balloons, markers, treasure (five pennies, five nickels, five dimes, five quarters), copies of the "Grandma's Treasure" handout (p. 123) and the "Family Covenant" handout (p. 123), chalk and chalkboard.

GATHERING ACTIVITY

Treasure Hunt

(up to 15 minutes)

For this activity, everyone will be together. Have everyone form four teams. Select one volunteer from each team to leave the room. Those who leave the room will be hunters. Escort the hunters out so there is no peeking. Give each team some treasure (one team gets pennies, another team gets dimes, and so forth). Instruct team members to hide the treasures somewhere in the room. When all coins are hidden, invite the hunters back in to search for the treasure.

Say: **You are on a treasure hunt! Other members of your team will give you temperature clues ("cold" means you're not even close; "warm" means you're getting closer) to guide you to the treasure you are to gather. Start hunting!**

Have the children in the teams guide the hunters to the treasure locations by yelling "Cold" if they are far away, and "Warm" or "Hot" if they are getting close. Each hunter listens to the temperature clues and searches until he or she finds all five of the team treasures, or until time is up. Keep the time limit to two or three minutes. Consider playing more than one round of this game, having teams select a different hunter each time.

Ask:

• **How did you feel as a hunter in this treasure hunt? as one who called out temperature tips?**

• **Like the treasure you sought in the hunt, what are some things that are hard to find? Explain.**

• **How is searching for people you can really look up to and be like similar to a treasure hunt? Why?**

Say: **Finding people we can look up to and be like can resemble a treasure hunt. Once you do find someone like this, you become much richer for it. There is a young man in the Bible named Timothy who had some great faith heroes he looked up to and wanted to be like. Let's look more closely at Timothy and his family today.**

BIBLE STORY TIME

Grandma's Treasure
(A Family Heritage)

(up to 15 minutes)

Say: Today we will learn about another kind of treasure—the kind that is most valuable and lasting, the treasure of a rich, close relationship with God. It is the treasure of faith in God that we model for those who come after us (such as children and grandchildren). Timothy's grandma, Lois, and his mother, Eunice, believed in Jesus and loved God very much. He so looked up to them and wanted to be like them that he grew to share their same faith and belief in Jesus Christ.

Families will work separately on this activity. Provide one copy of the "Grandma's Treasure" handout (p. 123) for each family. Families should read the page and write on their handouts their responses to the discussion questions. One parent or older child should lead the discussion in each family. After about ten minutes, have everyone gather for a short discussion. Ask:

• What are some highlights that were shared in your family discussion that this group may enjoy hearing or gain benefit from hearing?

• How did you feel as you discussed what your family was doing to pass along a sincere faith to others?

• What are some things we can do as families to better share our faith and show Christ's love to others?

Say: Paul, the one God used to write the verse on the handout, was Timothy's big "brother" in Christ. He wasn't actually related, but he was a positive role model. Paul was Timothy's hero, someone to look up to, and someone to be like. Like us, Timothy learned how to follow God by following others who followed God. Just as he looked up to Paul, Timothy looked up to and wanted to be like Lois and Eunice. Because of them, Timothy was able to mature in his faith because of the positive influence of his mother and grandmother. Each of us has the ability to influence others just as Lois and Eunice influenced Timothy.

FAMILY LEARNING ACTIVITY

Balloon Heroes

(up to 20 minutes)

Give each person an inflated balloon, a marker, scissors, and a quarter or half sheet of poster board. Welcome everyone.

Say: **Today we are going to learn how good examples have helped us or inspired us (and still are helping and inspiring us). To do this we will create Balloon Heroes to represent them. Begin by drawing on your balloon the face of someone you consider to be a good Christian example, someone you look up to and who you want to be like. Don't tell anyone who it is.**

Have families work separately while creating their Balloon Heroes. Each family should be seated around a table or at least in a circle of chairs. Encourage everyone to be creative and expressive. Parents should assist younger children with this activity.

After each person has drawn a balloon head to represent a hero, have each take a piece of poster board and make a small slit in the middle—just large enough for the tied end of the balloon to fit through. Each person should push the balloon mouth through the slot, using the poster board as a stand.

Say: **Now that you have a stand for your Balloon Hero, you are ready to start the next step. On the poster board stand for your Balloon Hero, write in large print the qualities you most like and admire about your hero. Write whatever you believe makes you look up to them or want to be like them. Some examples could be: "Knows the Word and lives it," "Loves others," "Always serving and helpful." Try to list at least four qualities. Continue to keep your hero's identity a secret. We will try to guess later.**

Allow groups up to ten minutes to work.

Gain everyone's attention and say: **Try to guess the identity of each Balloon Hero created by others in your family. Once someone guesses the correct identity of your hero, write the Balloon Hero's name in large letters on the poster board and your name on it in parentheses.**

When all the heroes have been guessed or identified, have people discuss the following questions within their families. Either write the following questions on the chalkboard or copy them for each family and distribute:

FOR Younger KIDS

During the Balloon Heroes activity, encourage adults to help children think of hero qualities. Young children might not quite grasp what wisdom is, so the specific example adults provide will be very helpful. For example, adults could point out heroic qualities as being things like "They make you feel good," "They encourage you," "They are very smart," "They are very loving," and "They have a happy attitude even when times are tough."

• Why did you choose this person as someone you most look up to or most want to be like? Who are they? How long have you known them?

• What qualities in them do you most respect and admire? Why?

• What are some specific things you believe you have learned from this person about faith? about other things?

After discussion, have families display their Balloon Heroes. Gain everyone's attention and say: **Walk around the room, and read the names and qualities of our heroes.** Allow three to five minutes for kids and parents to walk through the room and read the names and qualities of heroes. Ask:

• What did you learn as you read the names and qualities of heroes on our Balloon Heroes?

• What were some of the most unusual hero qualities you read?

• What were some hero qualities that really stuck out to you or that you saw a lot?

• Who would you consider to be your spiritual hero (or heroes)? Why?

• Who are some other people who are models of Christ for you or people who teach you spiritual things (such as the importance of prayer, service, and ministry)?

• In what ways have your family members served as models of Christ for you and helped you grow spiritually (examples might be: they pray with you, read the Bible with you, talk to you about spiritual things)?

Say: The example of Christ we model for others and the love and kindness we show, our activity in prayer and Bible reading—all of this is a treasure we have the privilege of passing on to others in our families and beyond. Just as we have received (and continue to receive) this treasure from others, we also have the responsibility to pass these treasures along to others.

COVENANT TIME

Heroic Examples

(up to 5 minutes)

Write the following questions on a chalkboard.

Say: As families, read 1 Timothy 4:12, and discuss the questions I've written on the board.

FOR Older KIDS

Encourage adults to allow older kids to help younger children with the Balloon Heroes activity. Older kids can help inflate the balloons, help tie the balloons off, and help children choose words to describe their heroes and write them on the poster board. This way, the older children can be heroes for the younger ones!

• In what ways can children be examples for adults? Try to give an example for each point in the verse: speech, life, love, faith, and purity.

• In what ways are people in our family a good example for others?

• In what one way could each of us be a better example of Christ and his love?

Say: The faith of Timothy's mother and grandmother was so sincere and so dynamic and strong that Timothy grew up to love God like they loved God. But you don't have to be a mother or grandmother to have a strong influence on others for Christ. If the Christians in the family will purpose to be "heroes" and faithfully live out Christ's character and show others Christ's love—showing love, faith, purity, and speaking kind words to each other—it will make a big difference.

Distribute one "Family Covenant" handout (p. 123) to each family, and say: Using the Family Covenant, decide on two or three ways that members of your family will agree to be strong examples of Christ and his love for others. Write this on your Covenant. Example: "We will say only words that are kind, loving, and pure."

Pray for each other to be willing and able to be positive examples in the areas noted on the Family Covenant.

OPTIONAL SNACK TIME

In advance, ask parents or grandparents to bring their favorite family dessert recipe (ideally one that has been passed down from a previous generation). Enjoy sampling each other's "Family Dessert Treasures."

EVALUATION

Because this is the final session, make sure you allow a few minutes to have parents and older students complete their evaluations. See page 125 for a copy-ready master of the evaluation form. A good time to have them complete these is during snack time. They will at least stay a few minutes to eat!

Grandma's Treasure

Instructions:

As a family, read the verse below. After reading the verse, discuss the questions that follow.

2 Timothy 1:5

"I have been reminded of your sincere faith, which first lived in your grandmother Lois and in your mother Eunice and, I am persuaded, now lives in you also."

Ask:

- How do you think a sincere faith was passed along to Timothy from his mother and grandmother? In light of this, how were Timothy's mother and grandmother heroes for him?

- What are some things people in our family have done that cause you to look up to them or want to be like them?

- What are some things others have done that have caused you to have more of a desire to participate in church, read your Bible, pray, serve, or minister to others? Explain.

- In what ways are our family members passing along sincere faith to one another? sharing Jesus with others?

- -

FAMILY COVENANT

To be even stronger examples of Christ, we the _____ family commit to:
(last name)

(Example: "Say only words that are kind, loving, and pure.")

- _____

- _____

- _____

Evaluation Form

Lesson Title_____   Date of Lesson_____

Please rate the following lesson components on a scale from one to five, with five being the highest.

• The Gathering Activity   _____

• The Bible Story Time   _____

• The Family Learning Activity   _____

• The Covenant Time   _____

• The overall session   _____

Things that could be improved:

_____

_____

_____

_____

_____

Things that went well:

_____

_____

_____

_____

_____

Other comments:

_____

_____

_____

_____

_____

Group Publishing, Inc.
Attention: Product Development
P.O. Box 481
Loveland, CO 80539
Fax: (970) 679-4370

Evaluation for
FAMILY SUNDAY SCHOOL FUN

Please help Group Publishing, Inc., continue to provide innovative and useful resources for ministry. Please take a moment to fill out this evaluation and mail or fax it to us. Thanks!

● ● ●

1. As a whole, this book has been (circle one)

not very helpful   very helpful

1   2   3   4   5   6   7   8   9   10

2. The best things about this book:

3. Ways this book could be improved:

4. Things I will change because of this book:

5. Other books I'd like to see Group publish in the future:

6. Would you be interested in field-testing future Group products and giving us your feedback? If so, please fill in the information below:

Name _____

Church Name _____

Denomination _____ Church Size _____

Church Address _____

City _____ State _____ ZIP _____

Church Phone _____

e-mail _____

Exciting Resources for Your Adult Ministry

Sermon-Booster Dramas

Tim Kurth

Now you can deliver powerful messages in fresh, new ways. Set up your message with memorable, easy-to-produce dramas—each just 3 minutes or less! These 25 low-prep dramas hit hot topics ranging from burnout…ethics…parenting…stress…to work…career issues and more! Your listeners will be on the edge of their seats!

ISBN 0-7644-2016-X

Fun Friend-Making Activities for Adult Groups

Karen Dockrey

More than 50 relational programming ideas help even shy adults talk with others at church! You'll find low-risk Icebreakers to get adults introduced and talking…Camaraderie-Builders that help adults connect and start talking about what's really happening in their lives…and Friend-Makers to cement friendships with authentic sharing and accountability.

ISBN 0-7644-2011-9

Bore No More (For Every Pastor, Speaker, Teacher)

Mike & Amy Nappa

This is a must-have for pastors, college/career speakers, and others who address groups! Because rather than just provide illustrations to entertain audiences, the authors show readers how to involve audiences in the learning process. The 70 sermon ideas presented are based on New Testament passages, but the principles apply to all passages.

ISBN 1-55945-266-8

Young Adult Faith-Launchers

These 18 in-depth Bible studies are perfect for young adults who want to strengthen their faith and deepen their relationships. They will explore real-world issues…ask the tough questions…and along the way turn casual relationships into supportive, caring friendships. Quick prep and high involvement make these the ideal studies for peer-led Bible studies, small groups, and classes.

ISBN 0-7644-2037-2

Bible Study Series

Give Your Teenagers a Solid Faith Foundation That Lasts a Lifetime!

Here are the *essentials* of the Christian life—core values teenagers *must* believe to make good decisions now...and build an *unshakable* lifelong faith. Developed by youth workers like you...field-tested with *real* youth groups in *real* churches...here's the meat your kids *must* have to grow spiritually—presented in a fun, involving way!

Each 4-session **Core Belief Bible Study Series** book lets you easily...

● Lead deep, compelling, *relevant* discussions your kids won't want to miss...

● Involve teenagers in exploring life-changing truths...

● Help kids create healthy relationships with each other—and you!

Plus you'll make an *eternal difference* in the lives of your kids as you give them a solid faith foundation that stands firm on God's Word.

Here are the Core Belief Bible Study Series titles already available...

Senior High Studies

Why **Authority** Matters	0-7644-0892-5
Why **Being a Christian** Matters	0-7644-0883-6
Why **Creation** Matters	0-7644-0880-1
Why **Forgiveness** Matters	0-7644-0887-9
Why **God** Matters	0-7644-0874-7
Why **God's Justice** Matters	0-7644-0886-0
Why **Jesus Christ** Matters	0-7644-0875-5
Why **Love** Matters	0-7644-0889-5
Why **Our Families** Matter	0-7644-0894-1
Why **Personal Character** Matters	0-7644-0885-2
Why **Prayer** Matters	0-7644-0893-3
Why **Relationships** Matter	0-7644-0896-8
Why **Serving Others** Matters	0-7644-0895-X
Why **Spiritual Growth** Matters	0-7644-0884-4
Why **Suffering** Matters	0-7644-0879-8
Why **the Bible** Matters	0-7644-0882-8
Why **the Church** Matters	0-7644-0890-9
Why **the Holy Spirit** Matters	0-7644-0876-3
Why **the Last Days** Matter	0-7644-0888-7
Why **the Spiritual Realm** Matters	0-7644-0881-X
Why **Worship** Matters	0-7644-0891-7

Junior High/Middle School Studies

The Truth About **Authority**	0-7644-0868-2
The Truth About **Being a Christian**	0-7644-0859-3
The Truth About **Creation**	0-7644-0856-9
The Truth About **Developing Character**	0-7644-0861-5
The Truth About **God**	0-7644-0850-X
The Truth About **God's Justice**	0-7644-0862-3
The Truth About **Jesus Christ**	0-7644-0851-8
The Truth About **Love**	0-7644-0865-8
The Truth About **Our Families**	0-7644-0870-4
The Truth About **Prayer**	0-7644-0869-0
The Truth About **Relationships**	0-7644-0872-0
The Truth About **Serving Others**	0-7644-0871-2
The Truth About **Sin and Forgiveness**	0-7644-0863-1
The Truth About **Spiritual Growth**	0-7644-0860-7
The Truth About **Suffering**	0-7644-0855-0
The Truth About **the Bible**	0-7644-0858-5
The Truth About **the Church**	0-7644-0899-2
The Truth About **the Holy Spirit**	0-7644-0852-6
The Truth About **the Last Days**	0-7644-0864-X
The Truth About **the Spiritual Realm**	0-7644-0857-7
The Truth About **Worship**	0-7644-0867-4